READY-TO-GO REPRODUCIBLES

Spelling

Puzzles & Mazes

By Jim Halverson

Grades 4–8

SCHOLASTIC
PROFESSIONAL BOOKS

New York • Toronto • London • Auckland • Sydney
Mexico City • New Delhi • Hong Kong • Buenos Aires

Dedication

My colleagues at Saint Ann's School asked for and inspired this book and its two companions, my students (no-nonsense editors!) enthusiastically helped me revise all three, and my family, dear Anita and Leif, supported and encouraged and often suffered through the writing process over several long years.

Cover design by Kelli Thompson
Interior design by Grafica, Inc.
Interior illustrations by Dave Clegg

ISBN 0-439-05187-8

Table of Contents

Introduction

What This Book Is...

The exercises in this book rest upon two assumptions: that students learn best when they are having fun, and that most students need frequent repetition of spelling concepts in order to retain them. These units are designed to help you address both needs. Instead of another spelling quiz to test and demonstrate their knowledge, the students get to solve puzzles, mazes, riddles, and picture mysteries.

The exercises are also designed to suit a range of teaching needs. They can be used by an entire class or for individual enrichment, and they reflect varying age and skills levels. Most units have three separate exercises, each a bit harder and more sophisticated than the one before it. You may find that only one is appropriate for the age level of the students you teach, or you may wish to work your way up through all of them.

You will also find an introductory page before each unit that summarizes and discusses the particular concept and offers a mini-lesson that can be used in several ways: to prepare students for the exercises, to review the concept after they have done the exercises, or to serve as a lead-in to your teaching of the concept.

...And Is Not

The introduction to each unit provides helpful rules, examples, teaching tips, and a mini-lesson. However, these introductions are not designed to be complete teaching guides. Similarly, the exercises are meant to supplement and enrich your teaching, not to provide a complete or methodical program for each concept. For easier spelling rules, you may find that the exercises here are sufficient, but for stubborn spelling problems, such as differentiating between plurals and possessives, you are surely going to want to build up to these exercises with preliminary work. You can then use these mazes and games as enjoyable rewards for mastering the concepts.

Before You Start...

Since the exercises require that students have a working knowledge of the concepts involved, it is very important for you to familiarize yourself with a unit before using it. Make sure that you have covered all the spelling decisions that crop up. Within the unit, check the degree of difficulty of the exercises and decide which pages best suit your students. Generally, the first page is probably best for fourth or fifth grade, the second for fifth or sixth, and the third for seventh or eighth, but these can be only very rough guidelines since classes vary so greatly.

...And After You Finish

I hope that you will connect the spelling activity pages in this book with real-world writing and help students see that an understanding of punctuation and capitalization is really just a small part of a bigger picture—written communication. The sooner they can make a spelling concept "theirs" by seeing it at work in their own writing, the sooner that spelling concept will be theirs for life. For instance, after students work on words with similar endings (Unit 13), you might give an assignment that asks them to write a story called "The Adventurous Octopus" in which they must use at least four more words ending with -ous and -us. Or have students proofread their writing like detectives searching for a certain spelling rule.

Finally, don't forget that good spelling is just one of many writing skills and not an end in itself. Some of your students—some of us!—are never going to be good spellers, but that should not prevent them from being appreciated as fine writers when their written communication is fresh, vivid, forceful, or delightful.

—Jim Halverson

Unit 1: Adding Prefixes and Suffixes to Root Words

Units 1–6 are designed to help students identify the *roots* of words and the *affixes* we attach to them in order to make many of our words in English.

Unit 1 addresses those affixes that we can add to root words without changing the root words. *Affixes* include *prefixes,* which come before the root, and *suffixes,* which come after it. For instance, we make the negative of the word *kind* by adding the prefix *un-* to it: *unkind.* If we want the noun form of *kind* instead of the adjective, we add the suffix *-ness* to it, making it *kindness.*

Rule: Generally, root words do not change when a prefix or suffix is added.

> **Examples:** *pre-* + view = preview
> forgive + *-ness* = forgiveness

Although there are frequent exceptions to this rule (see below), the basic rule makes it clear why we have double *n*'s and *l*'s in the word *unnaturally*: To the root word *natural* we have added the prefix *un-* and the suffix *-ly.*

Teaching Tip

Exceptions to the rule:

1. When the root word ends in a final silent *e* and we add a suffix starting with a vowel (*love + -able = lovable*)

2. When the word ends in a final *y* preceded by a consonant, we change the *y* to *i* before most suffixes.

3. When we double the final letter of some root words (*run + -ing = running*)

These exceptions are taken up in Unit 3 (final silent *e*), Unit 4 (final *y*) and Unit 5 (doubling). The exercises in this unit address only the basic rule and not the exceptions.

Mini-Lesson

When students learn to see the components of composite words, spelling becomes immediately less taxing. Instead of memorizing the entire sequence of letters in a word like *undoubtedly*, they can build the long word from relatively easy smaller units: *un + doubt + ed + ly*.

To help students understand root words and affixes, write a short word like *lock* on the board. Ask students to think of other words that can be built from that word—*locks*, *locked*, *locking*, *locker*, *unlock*. Do this with a few additional simple words that can be built on—*self*, *will*, *help*, and so on. Then write a composite word like *outfielder* and have them take it apart. Encourage students to use the terms *prefix*, *root word*, and *suffix* correctly.

Finally, students will enjoy a game of coining and defining their own funny new words by adding affixes to roots. Start them off with an example like *nonsleepover—what really happens when you have a friend stay over for the night.*

Answers

Page 7, Creating a Word Maker
Note: You may wish to enlarge this page to make it easier for students to use.

Page 8, Secret Message & Maze
(Secret Message) **1.** discoverable **2.** misspelled **3.** imperfect
4. enjoying **5.** arrangement **6.** goodness **7.** incorrect **8.** undone
9. slowly **10.** hopeless **11.** stubbornness **12.** thankful
Message: Very good work

(Maze) **The shortest path to the finish passes through**: **1.** unnoticed
2. personally **3.** misstated **4.** suddenness **5.** dissatisfy **6.** carefully
7. thinness

Page 9, Crossword Puzzle
Across: 4. immobile **6.** unnatural **10.** hopelessly **12.** dissatisfaction
14. stubbornness **15.** underrate **16.** lovely
Down: 1. illegally **2.** finally **3.** openness **5.** irresistible **8.** irrational
9. meanness **11.** naturally **13.** really * treat

Name _____ **Date** _____

Creating a Word Maker

A1
C3
B1
A2

E2
D1
D2
C1

Prefixes
dis H1
im B1
un A1

Root Words
enjoy F1
favor H2
fear D1
grace G1
happy A2
master E1
polite B2
wonder C1

Suffixes
able F2
ful C2, E2
less D2, G2

Directions: Copy the prefixes, root words, and suffixes in the spaces that match the code after them. Each first letter should be placed above the line which is underlined. As an example, H1 has been put in for you. Then follow the directions for cutting and folding the page to make the words come together.

F2
E1
F1
C2

G1
B2
H2
D I S H1

Directions: If you know how to fold a piece of paper into a "fortune teller," then you can use the same technique for this word maker.

(1) After cutting the paper where indicated to make a square, give yourself some guidelines by neatly folding the paper in half in each direction and along each diagonal.

(2) Unfold the paper, place it with the printed side facing down, and fold each corner to the center.

(3) Turn the new square over and repeat the process of (2), folding each corner to the center. Now all of the letters that you wrote on the page should be visible.

(4) After creasing again along the center lines to make guides, pull up the flaps on the unprinted side of the square and insert your thumb and three fingers into the four cavities. Bring your fingers together so that the four corners meet at one point.

(5) When you open the figure one way, you'll find that you have created one set of words, and when you open it the other way, it will make a second set.

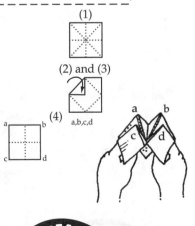

(1)

(2) and (3)

(4) a,b,c,d

a   b

c   d

a   b

c   d

Name _____ Date _____

Secret Message & Maze

Directions: Each clue defines a word for you to write in the given spaces. All the words can be built from the lists of root words, prefixes, and suffixes. When you have finished, a secret message will appear in the vertical box. The first one has been done for you.

Hint: You may use the prefixes and suffixes more than once, but only use each root word once!

Clues

1. If something can be found, it is _____.

2. When words are written incorrectly, they are _____.

3. Something which has flaws is _____.

4. When you're having fun, you're _____ yourself.

5. The way things are placed is their _____.

6. The opposite of evil is _____.

7. If something is wrong it is _____.

8. When your shoelaces aren't tied, they are _____.

9. A turtle moves very _____.

10. When everything looks terrible, things seem _____.

11. People who refuse to change their minds show _____.

12. If you are grateful, you are _____.

1 d i s c o v e r a b l e
2 _ _ _ _ _ _ _ _ _
3 _ _ _ _ _ _ _
4 _ _ _ _ _ _ _
5 _ _ _ _ _ _ _ _ _
6 _ _ _ _ _ _
7 _ _ _ _ _ _ _
8 _ _ _ _ _ _
9 _ _ _ _ _ _
10 _ _ _ _ _
11 _ _ _ _ _ _ _ _ _
12 _ _ _ _ _ _ _

Prefixes
dis-   en-   im-   in-   mis-   un-

Root Words
arrange	correct	✓cover
done	good	hope
joy	perfect	slow
spell	stubborn	thank

Suffixes
-able   -ed   -er   -ful   -ing
-less   -ly   -ment -ness

Maze

Directions: Find the shortest path to the finish by passing through only seven correctly spelled words. Avoid misspelled words—incorrect words act as blocks! Be careful: Some paths lead to dead ends.

suddenness

unatural   misstated   dissatisfy   stubborness

START   personally   realy   carefully   FINISH

unnoticed   immature   mispelling   thinness

usually

8

READY-TO-GO REPRODUCIBLES

Crossword Puzzle

Name _____ **Date** _____

Directions: Add an affix to each of the root words in the box below to help you solve the clues and complete the crossword puzzle. One clue has been done for you.

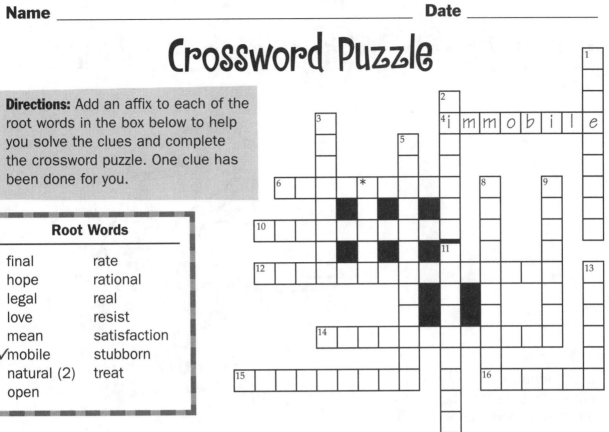

Root Words

final	rate
hope	rational
legal	real
love	resist
mean	satisfaction
✓mobile	stubborn
natural (2)	treat
open	

Across

4. If you can't move something, it is
   _____immobile_____.

6. Artificial food that is made in a machine is _____.

10. When you think everything will go wrong, you are thinking _____.

12. A groan is an expression of
    _____.

14. Someone who refuses to give in shows _____.

15. When you give too low a value to something, you _____ it.

16. If something is beautiful, it is
    _____.

Down

1. If you break the law, you are acting
   _____.

2. If you receive something after a long wait, you might say, "_____!"

3. If your mind is not closed, you are showing
   _____.

5. Something that you just have to have is
   _____.

8. Ideas that do not make sense are
   _____.

9. Misers and nasty people are known for their _____.

11. If you react the way people always do, you are acting _____.

13. Another word for *truly* is _____.

* If you have completed this puzzle correctly, you deserve a _____.

Unit 2: Plurals: Adding -s, -es, and -ies

Unit 2 introduces students to affixes that change when they are attached to certain words, and to root words that change when we add certain affixes to them.

We use the suffix *-s* for two reasons in English: We add it to most singular nouns to make them plural (*bird* becomes *birds*), and we add it to verbs when we use the third person singular of the present tense (*I* or *you sing* but **she** *sings*). Most of the time, when adding -s to root words, we follow the basic rule for adding affixes: Keep the root word the same and simply add the -s.

However, the *-s* becomes *-es* when added to certain nouns and verbs and *-ies* when added to others.

Rule 1: We add -es instead of -s when a noun or verb ends in *ch*, *sh*, *x*, *ss*, or *z*: *church–churches; crush–crushes; fox–foxes; miss–misses; buzz–buzzes.*

Rule 2: When a noun or verb ends in a final *y*, we change the *y* to *i* and add -es: *canary–canaries; fly–flies.*

Spelling Puzzles & Mazes • Scholastic Professional Books

Teaching Tips

★ When adding -es instead of -s, most people don't even think about the consonants that end the root words; they just hear that those consonants force us to add another syllable, making the final s sound more like a z: *bush-ez*, not the almost unpronounceable *bush-s*. Some students benefit from having this pointed out.

★ You'll find more help with final *y* words in Unit 4, which is devoted exclusively to the final *y* rule.

Mini-Lesson

After going over this rule in preparation for the activities that follow, you can reinforce the concepts and at the same time provide a nice break for the students with a short exercise that brings them up to the board. Give each student a sticky-note that can be attached to the board or a prepared poster. Each square should have an ending written on it: -s, -es, or -ies. For each student in the class, write a singular word, some that require an -s, some that require an -es, and some that need -ies to make their plurals. Students then bring up their endings, individually or in small groups, and each finds an appropriate word and sticks the ending onto it. (In the case of the -ies endings, they will of course have to stick them over the final *y* of the root word.)

Answers

Page 12, What's Wrong With This Picture?
Words that end in -s: signs, snacks, toys, months, decoys
Words that end in -es: brushes, mixes, pouches, couches, foxes, dishes
Words that end in -ies: flies, cookies, supplies, puppies, kitties

Page 13, Grid & Maze
(Grid) 1. churches **2.** taxes **3.** ponies **4.** plays **5.** flosses **6.** buzzes **7.** cliffs **8.** kitties **9.** flashes **10.** lights **11.** matches **12.** dresses **13.** fixes **14.** candies

(Maze) The shortest path to the finish goes through: 1. passes **2.** nights **3.** dishes **4.** bosses **5.** mixes **6.** buzzes **7.** ladies **8.** latches **9.** trays **10.** misses **11.** dashes **12.** ditches **13.** buys **14.** clocks **15.** taxes **16.** babies **17.** parties **18.** wishes
Bonus: boxes

Name _____ Date _____

What's Wrong With This Picture?

Directions: Herman Hound is a smart and successful storekeeper, but he sure needs help spelling plurals! Herman knows that you usually add -s to the singular form but that sometimes you must add -es or change the final y of a word to i and then add -es. Help Herman by finding and correcting 16 misspelled plurals in his store.

Magazines and Books

Dog Life · Teen Puppys · Doghouse Beautiful · Canine Digest

Twelve Monthes in the Doghouse · Couchs Are for Sleeping

Mad Dogs and Englishmen · Kittys Beware!

A Bird in the Bushes · Outfoxing Foxs

Warning Signes

Beware the Owner

Skunks Crossing

Danger: Porcupines

Snackes

Trail Mixs · Human Being Crackers

Kitten Kisses · Cat Cookys

Bath Toies

Combs and Brushs

Grooming Department

Powders for Fleas, Ticks, and Flys

Collars and Leashes

Bowls and Dishs

Hunting Supplys

Duck Decoies · Earplugs

Backpacks and Pouchs · Sweaters

READY·TO·GO REPRODUCIBLES

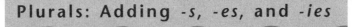

Name _____ **Date** _____

Grid & Maze

Directions: Fit the words in the box into the grid puzzle by writing them in their plural forms (add the appropriate ending: -s, -es, or -ies). Make sure that each word fits in exactly— that there are no unused spaces. One letter of each word has been written in for you to help you tell where each word belongs, and number 10 has been filled in for you.

1. C _ _ _ _ _ _ _

2. _ a _ _ _ _

3. _ _ n _ _ _ _

4. _ _ _ y _

5. _ _ o _ _ _ _

6. _ u _ _ _ _

7. _ _ _ f _ _

8. _ i _ _ _ _ _ _

9. _ l _ _ _ _ _ _

10. l i g h t s

11. m _ _ _ _ _ _

12. _ _ e _ _ _ _

13. _ i _ _ _ _

14. _ _ n _ _ _ _
        ?

buzz	floss
candy	kitty
church	✓ light
cliff	match
dress	play
fix	pony
flash	tax

Maze

Directions: Find the shortest path to the finish by passing through 18 correctly spelled words. You cannot pass through a solid line or an area containing a misspelled word. Be careful! Some paths lead to dead ends.

☀ **Bonus:** What is the one correctly spelled word that is not in the path? _____

START ... churchs ... mixes ... passes ... nights ... buzzes ... dishes ... ladies ... roastes ... bosses ... reportes ... boxes ... latches ... pillowes ... wishes ... trys ... pushs ... parties ... FINISH ... trays ... roachs ... ditches ... misses ... babies ... sighes ... taxes ... clocks ... buys ... enemys ... dashes

Unit 3: The Final Silent *e* Rule

Unit 3 focuses on root words that change when suffixes are added to them. When adding suffixes that begin with vowels to root words that end in a final silent *e*, we drop the final *e* to avoid a possibly confusing vowel combination. Thus, adding *-able* to *use* gives us *usable*, instead of the more awkward *useable*.

Note that the letter *y* serves as a vowel when it is pronounced like long *e* or long *i*. Thus the *e* is dropped when adding the suffix *y* to words like *taste* or *spice: tasty, spicy*.

> **The Final Silent *e* Rule:**
>
> **When a root word ends in a final silent e:**
>
>   **(1) Drop the *e* before suffixes that begin with a vowel.**
>
>   **(2) Keep the *e* before suffixes that begin with a consonant.**

Teaching Tip

Exceptions to the rule:

1. Words that end in *-ce* or *-ge* often keep the final e before the vowels *a*, *o*, and *u* so that the c and g sounds remain soft—*noticeable, manageable*.

2. Words that end in a vowel followed by silent e—*canoeing (canoe), tying (tie), truly (true), argument (argue)*.

3. The words *awful, ninth*, and *wholly*.

These exceptions do not appear in the exercises in this unit.

Spelling Puzzles & Mazes • Scholastic Professional Books

Mini-Lesson

Since students remember spelling rules best when they understand why they came to be, it is good to emphasize the reason that the silent *e* was invented in the first place: to signal that the preceding vowel is long. You can make this learning fun by playing a little game on the board. Write a word like *hopeless* and ask a student to pronounce it and tell you what it means. Now cross out the silent *e* and rewrite the word as *hopless*. Tell the students that *h-o-p-l-e-s-s* isn't a real word, but if it were, how would it be pronounced and what would it mean? Now write *hoping* and ask why that *o* is long, making it pronounced *hoping* and not *hopping*. Make sure they see that the vowel-consonant-vowel combination signals a long *o* in the root word.

Try the same again with another word: without the *e*, *careful* becomes *carful*. Make sure that the students hear the difference. Then add *caring,* emphasizing that it is built on the root word *care*, not *car*. Finally, see if students can come up with similar examples themselves.

Answers

Page 16, Secret Message & Maze
(Message) Correctly spelled words: 1. yoking **2.** oozing **3.** useless **4.** wholeness **5.** offensively **6.** ripeness **7.** knavish **8.** entirely **9.** desirable **10.** wakeful **11.** extremely **12.** lovable **13.** likeness
Secret message: *You worked well.*

(Maze) The shortest path to the finish passes through: 1. coming **2.** lovable **3.** hopeful **4.** famous **5.** surely **6.** voting **7.** adorable **8.** rareness **9.** sharing **10.** careless **11.** placement **12.** whistling **13.** wholeness **14.** priceless
Bonus: 21; all the above plus Start, Finish, riding, hateful, nicely, tasty, shameful

Page 17, Tongue Twisters
Misspelled words: 1. sliding, slimy **2.** sharing, shiny **3.** brutish, bruising **4.** grimy, griping **5.** Terribly, taking, timelessly, tiresome

Page 18, Crossword Puzzle
Across: 1. measurements **6.** tracing **7.** scary **8.** creative **11.** tiresome **13.** careful **14.** gesturing **15.** useful **17.** wisely **18.** lovable **19.** movement **20.** spicy
Down: 2. extremely **3.** noticing **4.** shamelessly **5.** desirable **9.** troublesome **10.** voting **12.** safety **16.** surely

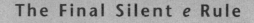

The Final Silent *e* Rule

Name _____ **Date** _____

Secret Message & Maze

Directions: Hidden in the string of words below is a secret message. Find it by circling the first letter of every word that is spelled correctly. The first letter of the message has been circled for you as an example.

comeingfinly**l**okingmeasurmentoozingtasteylatlyuselesswholenesshorribley-
tuneingoffensivelyripenessmanagmentpleaseuredivinlyknavishbiteingen-
tirelyadoreabledesirablemovmentlatnessforgiveingwakefulniclyextremelylov-
ablerequirmentvoteinglikenessexcitmentpossibley

Maze

Directions: Find the shortest path to the finish by passing through 14 correctly spelled words. You cannot pass through a solid line or an area containing an incorrectly spelled word. Be careful! Some paths lead to dead ends!

⭐ **Bonus:** How many correctly spelled words, including Start and Finish, are there in the entire maze?

_____

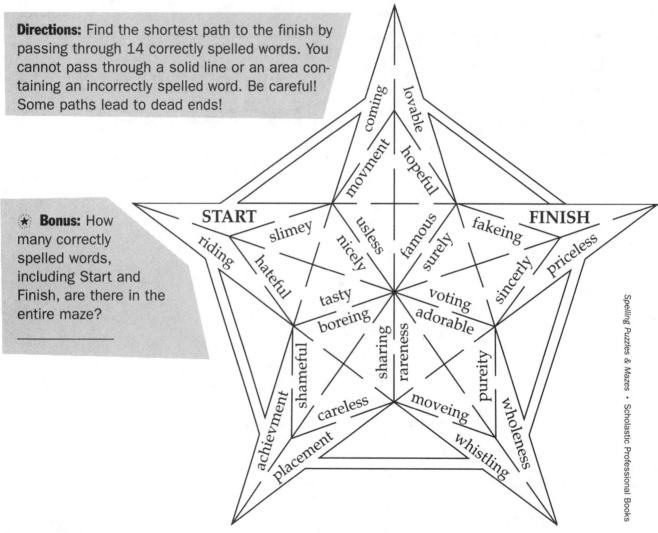

Spelling Puzzles & Mazes • Scholastic Professional Books

Name _____ **Date** _____

Tongue Twisters

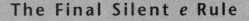

Alliteration is the repetition of a beginning consonant sound, like the *f* sound in **French-fried frogs**. A *tongue twister* is a sentence or phrase with alliteration and alternating sounds that make it difficult to say quickly.

Directions: The lines below are full of alliteration, and they contain lots of final silent e rule spelling errors! See if you can find and correct all 12 mistakes. Write the corrections over the incorrectly spelled words. When you've finished, create some tongue twisters of your own.

1. Slick sloppy slideing with a slimey slippery sled stinks.

2. Surely shy Shirley is shareing her shiney shells.

3. A bruteish brigand was bruiseing and breaking his brown bread.

4. The grimey, gripeing grandmother grabbed the greasy green griddle.

5. Terribley tall Thomas was takeing his timlessly tuneful tapes to tiny, tirsome Titus.

Make up a few of your own tongue twisters!

_____

_____

_____

_____

_____

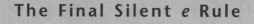

Name _____ Date _____

Crossword Puzzle

Directions: The answers to all the clues are words that follow the final silent *e* rule. Add suffixes to the root words from the box below to find the answers. Each root word may be used only once. The first one has been done for you.

Root Words		
care	move	tire
create	notice	trace
desire	safe	trouble
extreme	scare	use
gesture	shame	vote
love	spice	wise
✓measure	sure	

Across

1. Things that you make with a ruler are <u>measurements</u>.

6. Thin paper can be placed over a design to make a _____.

7. Suspense movies are often very _____.

8. An imaginative and original artist is _____.

11. A boring person can be called this: _____.

13. If you are not reckless, you are _____.

14. You can communicate without words by _____.

15. If a tool helps you in many ways, it is _____.

17. People who make smart choices are acting _____.

18. Another word for *adorable* is _____.

19. This is part of a symphony or another word for motion. _____

20. A dish made with hot peppers is _____.

Down

2. If you are very, very hungry, you are _____ hungry.

3. If you are very observant, you are _____ what is around you.

4. People who intentionally act in embarrassing ways are acting _____.

5. Something that you want is _____.

9. If something worries you, it is _____.

10. On election day, people use machines for this: _____.

12. If you are watching out for danger, you are thinking about _____.

16. This is a synonym of *certainly*: _____.

18

Spelling Puzzles & Mazes • Scholastic Professional Books

Unit 4: The Final *y* Rule

Unit 4 continues the lesson on root words that change, focusing on adding suffixes to root words that end in *y*.

In words like *try*, *marry*, and *silly*, where the final *y* of the root word is preceded by a consonant, we change the *y* to *i* before adding the suffix—*tried*, *marriage*, and *silliness*. However, if the final *y* is preceded by a vowel, as in *play* and *buoy*, there is no change— *playful*, *buoyant*. Also, when adding a suffix that begins with *i*, like *-ing*, we always keep the final *y* to avoid an awkward double *i*—*try* + *-ing* = *trying* not *triing*.

The Final *y* Rules:

1. When a root word ends in a consonant and then *y*, change the *y* to *i* before all suffixes except those that begin with *i*.

2. When a root word ends in a vowel and then *y*, do not change the *y* before any suffix.

Teaching Tips

★ There are, luckily, very few exceptions to the rule (such as *ladylike* and *daily*). No exceptions are included in the exercises that follow.

★ One complicating factor (already treated in Unit 2) is that in order to add *-s* to a word ending in a consonant and a *y*, we must also add an *e* before the final *s*: *fly* becomes *flies* not *flis*, so that we won't pronounce a short *i* like in the word *this*. (You may wish to have students do the exercises in Unit 2 before tackling those that follow.)

Mini-Lesson

This rule demands that students look at the letter before the final *y* of the root word, and a discovery session is a good way to stress this idea. Ask the students to pretend that they're detectives. Write two groups of words on the board, one in which the final *y* of the root words must be changed to *i* before adding a suffix other than *-ing*, and one in which the final *y* is not changed. Can students find a clue in the root words that always lets them know if the *y* should be changed to *i*? Then write models like the following, for now avoiding the *-ing* ending:

toy–toys	try–tried
pray–prayer	marry–marriage
joy–joyous	sunny–sunnier

After some false starts and a little direction, the students will notice that all the words that keep the *y* have a vowel before it; those that change to *i* are preceded by a conso-nant. You can then add in the *-ing* exception and ask why a word like *marrying* keeps the *y* while *married* does not. Students will quickly notice the odd double *i* combination of the spelling *marriing*.

Answers

Page 21, Hidden Message
1. plentiful (t) **2.** loneliness (s) **3.** pitiless (i) **4.** drying (y) **5.** joyful (f)
6. babies (b) **7.** stayed (a) **8.** silliness (l) **9.** sunnier (e) **10.** happier (p)
11. crazily (z) **12.** lovelier (v)
Message: RAIN

Page 22, Maze
The shortest path to the finish passes through: 1. grayer **2.** donkeys
3. played **4.** flies **5.** craziest **6.** angrier **7.** sunnier **8.** happiness
9. countries **10.** prayed
Bonus: 30; all the above plus Start, Finish, funniest, trying, destroyer, merrily, denying, dizziness, joyful, buying, replied, trays, flying, cried, payment, tinier, married, carried, sleepily, parties

Name _____   **Date** _____

Hidden Message

The Lee family is planning to have a party on their patio. If only they could read the message in the flagstones, however, they might change their minds! Help them learn why they should make other plans by completing the puzzle.

Directions: Using the final *y* rule, spell out the answers to the clues below. After you have filled in the missing word in each sentence, shade in the flagstones that match the circled letters in the answer grid. As an example, the first word has been given for you, and the flagstone containing the letter *t* has been shaded in.

Hints: The root words for the clue answers are in this box, but you must add endings to them before they will answer the clues. Use each root word only once!

baby	joy	✓plenty
crazy	lonely	silly
dry	love	stay
happy	pity	sunny

Clues

1. When there is a large amount of something, it is p l e n t i f u l .

2. If you are by yourself but wish to be with others, you are experiencing __ __ __ __ __ __ __ __ __ [ ] .

3. Someone who has no feelings for a person in pain is __ __ __ [ ] __ __ __ .

4. Wet clothes hanging on a line in the sun are __ __ __ [ ] __ __ .

5. People who are full of happiness are __ __ __ [ ] __ __ .

6. Newborn children are [ ] __ __ __ __ __ .

7. Another word for *remained* is __ __ [ ] __ __ __ .

8. Clowns are known for their humor and __ __ __ [ ] __ __ __ __ __ .

9. When clouds start to go away, the day becomes __ __ __ __ __ [ ] __ .

10. The opposite of *sadder* is __ __ [ ] __ __ __ __ .

11. People behaving in a mad way are acting __ __ __ [ ] __ __ __ .

12. A word that means *more beautiful* is __ __ [ ] __ __ __ __ .

Name _____ Date _____

Maze

Directions: Find the shortest path to the finish by passing through 10 correctly spelled words. You cannot pass through a solid line or an area containing an incorrectly spelled word. Be careful! Some paths lead to dead ends.

✴ **Bonus:** How many correctly spelled words, including Start and Finish, are there in the entire maze? _____

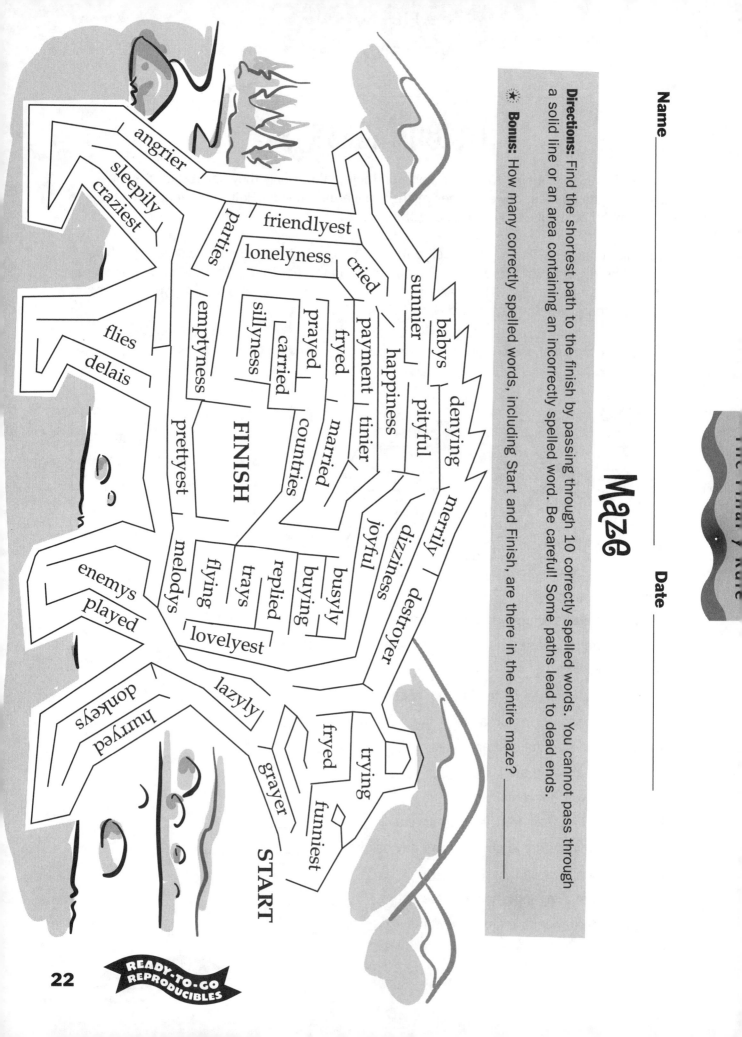

angrier
sleepily
craziest
friendlyest
lonelyness
parties
emptyness
sillyness
carried
prayed
fryed
payment
cried
sunnier
happiness
pityful
babys
denying
merrily
flies
delais
prettyest
melodys
countries
married
tinier
dizziness
destroyer
joyful
busyly
buying
replied
trays
flying
lovelyest
FINISH
enemys
played
lazyly
fryed
trying
funniest
grayer
hurryed
donkeys
START

READY-TO-GO REPRODUCIBLES

Unit 5: The One-Syllable Doubling Rule

Units 5 and 6 focus on the last of the cases that call for changing root words when adding suffixes: the need to double the final consonant of some words. This unit addresses doubling the final consonant of one-syllable words; unit 6 presents the case of two-syllable words.

We double the final consonant of one-syllable root words only when we are adding a suffix that begins with a vowel—*run* becomes *running*; *bat* becomes *batter*. If the suffix begins with a consonant, then the two consonants keep the vowel of the root word soft and there is no need to double. Consider *winner* and *winless*. If we didn't double the *n* in the first case—*wining*—then the word would be pronounced like *whining*. However, we don't need to double the *n* in *winless* because the final *n* of *win* combined with the initial *l* of *less* keeps the *i* short. Similarly, if the root word itself ends in two consonants, like the word *start*, then we don't need to double the final *t* to make *starting*.

Finally, if the one-syllable root word has a two-vowel combination, then the vowel sound is maintained by the combination, and the final consonant does not need to be doubled—*need* becomes *needed*; *soon* becomes *sooner*; *read* becomes *reading*.

The Doubling Rule for One-Syllable Words: If a one-syllable root word ends with a single consonant that is preceded by a single vowel, double the final consonant when adding a suffix that begins with a vowel.

Teaching Tip

Exceptions to the rule:

1. A final *x* is not doubled: *mix* becomes *mixed*.

2. Several other infrequently used final consonants are not doubled: *c, h, k, j, q, v, w*.

3. The final *s* of *bus* is not doubled—*bus* becomes *busing*.

4. The *u* of the *qu* combination does not act like a vowel—*quit* becomes *quitting*.

None of these exceptions are included in the exercises of this unit.

Mini-Lesson

Help students understand that doubling the final consonant of one-syllable root words according to this rule helps us to pronounce words correctly: Without this rule, words like *running* and *batter* would be written *runing* and *bater,* and might be pronounced as *roo-ning* and *bay-ter*, with long *u* and *a* sounds. The doubling also prevents confusion with root words whose final *e* has been dropped because of the final silent *e* rule (Unit 3)— *starring* and *staring*; *diner* and *dinner*. To reinforce the rule, keep students thinking about how single and double consonants influence the vowels that precede them. Write pairs of words like *fury* and *furry* on the board and ask the students to pick the word that fits the sentence you dictate. Or, as in the pairs below, ask them to say what the sentence would mean with each word. These are pairs that students can have fun with:

- When I get home, I'm going to eat a huge (diner, dinner).
- The actress (stared, starred) in her last two movies.
- I think I've been (robed, robbed)!
- Your speakers have a (tiny, tinny) sound.
- I was (scared, scarred) in the fun house!

Answers

Page 25, What's Wrong With This Picture?
Words that should have double letters: 1. upper **2.** cutters
3. clippers **4.** swimming **5.** running **6.** funny **7.** slippers **8.** shopping
9. winner **10.** chopped **11.** canned **12.** hottest
Words that should not have double letters: 1. waiting **2.** super
3. seedless **4.** greenest

Page 26, Maze
The path to the finish passes through 1. cutting **2.** swimmer
3. starry **4.** saddest **5.** clammy **6.** planned **7.** getting **8.** bigger
Corrected spellings: slipped, beaten, funny

Page 27, Help the Poet
Misspellings: 1. getting **2.** fretful **3.** setting **4.** daddy **5.** getting
6. skinny **7.** pouted **8.** running **9.** napping **10.** snapped **11.** meany
12. sobbed **13.** planned **14.** manly **15.** stepped **16.** chatter **17.** grinner
18. witty **19.** witty **20.** potter **21.** dragged **22.** sporty **23.** wedding
24. hugged **25.** grabbed

What's Wrong With This Picture?

The people who make the signs in Spellville aren't very good spellers, or perhaps they just never learned the doubling rule. Usually they forget to double the final consonant of a root word when adding a suffix to it, but a few times they have doubled letters that should not be doubled.

Directions: See if you can find 16 spelling errors in the picture below. Write the words correctly in the appropriate spaces.

Words that should have double letters:

1. _____
2. _____
3. _____
4. _____
5. _____
6. _____
7. _____
8. _____
9. _____
10. _____
11. _____
12. _____

Words that should not have double letters:

1. _____
2. _____
3. _____
4. _____

Hairy Harry's BARBER SHOP

Old-Fashioned Hair Cuters
No Electric Clipers Used!

Women, Men, and
Children Welcome

Shaves and
Shampoos

Uper Main St.

We're Fast!
No Waitting!

Cute & Chic CLOTHIERS

Biggest Bargains!

Hot Pants and Cool Shorts

All Sizes of Swiming Suits

Suits and Dresses

Walking and Runing Shoes

Silly Socks and Funy Hats

Soft Bathrobes and Slipers

Supper Sales!

MAIN STREET · MARKET ·

Today's Specials

Choped Meat— $2.49 lb.

Whole Chickens— $1.99 lb.

All Caned Fruit— $.50

Pitted Olives— $1.09 lb.

Hotest Hot Peppers— $.79 each

Seeddless Grapefruit— $.39 each

Strawberries— $2.29 qt.

The Greennest
Green Beans— $.49 lb.

Paper Towels— $.99 roll

Contest!
Ten minutes of
free shoping!
Come in and
be a winer!

Name_____ **Date** _____

Maze

Directions: Find the shortest path to the finish by passing through eight correctly spelled words. You cannot pass through a solid line or an area containing a misspelled word.

⭐ **Bonus:** There are three incorrectly spelled words in the maze. Write the correct spelling of these words in the box provided at the bottom of the page.

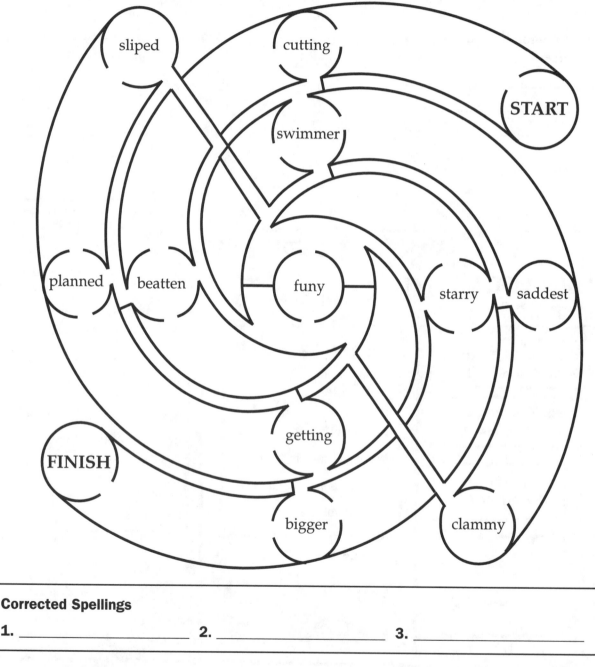

Corrected Spellings

1. _____ 2. _____ 3. _____

Spelling Puzzles & Mazes • Scholastic Professional Books

Name_____ **Date**_____

Help the Poet

Directions: The writer of this little poem has made 25 doubling-rule spelling mistakes. Find as many of them as you can and write the correct spellings in the blanks to the left. In the first two stanzas, look for *possible* errors in the underlined words; after that you must find the mistakes for yourself.

Penny Potter's Comeuppance

_____ The day was hot and <u>geting</u> <u>hotter</u>
_____ As Potter, the <u>potter,</u> and his <u>frettful</u> daughter,
_____ Pretty Penny,
_____ Were <u>seting</u> up at a small county fair.

_____ "I wish some smart and handsome <u>laddie</u>
_____ Would waltz me away from this <u>draggy</u> <u>dady</u>,"
_____ Thought Penny;
_____ "If he bugs me he'd better beware!"

_____ "I'm hot, I'm tired, I'm geting skiny—
_____ He knows nothing but work, that old bald ninny,"
_____ Poutted Penny,
_____ And she dreamed about runing away.

_____ "I caught you naping, you slothful shirker.
_____ You must work—like a Trojan, a fiend, a berserker!"
_____ Snaped Potter.
_____ "You'll be sad if you dally today."

_____ "I'll show you, you meanny, you miney, you moe!
_____ 'Potter's Pots' is *your* life—*I'm* going to go!"
_____ Sobed Penny,
_____ And their lives changed—but not as she'd planed.

Help the Poet (continued)

_____ For at just that moment a mannly mister

_____ Named Stanley Panner steped up and kissed her,

_____ Kissed Penny,

_____ On the hand, of course, just on her hand.

_____ A nodder and chater, a winker and griner,

_____ Stan was charming and wity and surely a winner,

_____ Thought Penny.

_____ Thought Potter: Wity, but surely a jerk!

_____ Stan saw that the poter was less than impressed

_____ By the span of his smile and the breadth of his chest.

_____ Thought Panner:

_____ This Potter loves love less than work.

_____ So Stanley then draged from his sportty sedan

_____ A piece of *his* work—an immense copper pan.

_____ Gasped Potter,

_____ "We must publish the glad weding banns."

_____ Penny huged Stanley and wished for true bliss,

_____ Stanley grabed Penny and wished for a kiss.

_____ Wished Potter:

_____ In red—POTTER'S POTS *AND PANS*.

Word Glossary

Several of the words in the poem may be new to you. Here are brief definitions.

comeuppance—(informal) Deserved punishment; getting what one truly deserves.

slothful—Lazy; acting like a *sloth*, a mammal in the bear family known for inactivity.

shirker—Someone who *shirks*, i.e., who puts off or avoids doing work.

berserker—A warrior in Norse mythology known for fierce, frenzied fighting.

banns (sometimes spelled *bans*)— Formal announcements in church of an intended wedding.

Unit 6: The Two-Syllable Doubling Rule

 **traveler**

This unit covers the two-syllable doubling rule, which is simply an extension of the one-syllable doubling rule covered in Unit 5. The two-syllable doubling rule also deals with the problem of adding suffixes that begin with vowels to words that end in a single consonant preceded by a single vowel. In this case, however, the root word has two syllables, and the spelling of the final word depends on where the stress (also called the *accent*) falls.

If the stress falls on the first syllable of the root word, as in *traveler*, we don't need to double the final consonant of the root word. (One wouldn't be tempted to mispronounce *traveler* as *traVEELer* since the second syllable isn't stressed.)

If, however, the stress falls on the second syllable, as in *repelled*, then we do double the final consonant of the root word when adding the suffix that begins with a vowel—*repel* becomes *repelled*. (If we didn't double the *l* and spelled the word *repeled*, then it might seem as if we should pronounce it like *repealed*.)

The Doubling Rule for Two-Syllable Words: Double the final consonant of a two-syllable root word when adding a suffix that begins with a vowel ONLY IF:

(a) the stress falls on the second syllable of the root word,

AND

(b) the root word ends in a single consonant preceded by a single vowel.

Teaching Tip

Exceptions to the rule:

1. In British spelling the final consonant is usually doubled even if the accent of the root word is on the first syllable. Most American dictionaries include alternate spellings of these words—*traveller, pedalled, worshipping*—but you cannot count on words in this category having an alternate—*offering* would be incorrect.

2. There are only very rare alternatives if the accent falls on the second syllable, like *chagrined*, and you won't be wrong if you consistently double the final consonant.

The exercises in this unit follow the rule strictly with no examples of alternative spellings.

Mini-Lesson

Identifying where the stress falls in multisyllabic words is a very easy process for some students but a very frustrating one for others. Help everyone master the skill by first looking at familiar multisyllabic words, like their first, middle, or last names (or the names of favorite celebrities and sports heroes).

After a short training session, go around the room and have students orally identify the accented syllables in their own names or other names they've selected. Demonstrate how to find the stress by overpronouncing syllables. For names like *Tanya*, for example, say, "Is it pronounced **TAN**-ya or tan-**YA**?" Then you might show how the names *Mary* and *Marie* are really made up of the same sounds with different syllables stressed. When you ask students to identify the stress in their names, have them use this overpronunciation technique to "prove" where the accent falls. This will especially help those students who have difficulty hearing accents. After this work, let students exaggerate the stresses in less familiar words, like *referred* and *offering*.

Answers

Page 31, Solve the Riddle

1. committed, rebelling, controlled, dispelling, submitted
2. transmitted, totaled, profited, flickered **3.** upsetting, preferred, canceled, deferred, transferring **4.** whimpering, wavered, permitting, traveling
Answer to the riddle: One mends his sail, and the other sends his mail.

Page 32, Maze
The shortest path to the finish passes through: 1. admitted
2. canceled **3.** utterance **4.** patrolled **5.** devilish **6.** occurrence
7. regretted **8.** upsetting **9.** reference **10.** propeller **11.** entered
12. transferring **13.** totaling **14.** committee **15.** permitted **16.** opener
17. galloped **18.** submitting **19.** suffered **20.** forgettable
21. repellent **22.** profited **23.** controlling **24.** different **25.** referring
Bonus: 31; all the above plus Start, Finish, traveled, expelled, conference, deferred

Name_____ **Date** _____

Solve the Riddle

What's the difference between a sailor doing a sewing job and a man posting a letter?

Directions: To solve the riddle, you must fit all of the root words from the box into the grid. But the grid is made for the words to go in with an *-ed* or *-ing* ending; thus you have to decide if by adding that ending you must double the final consonant of the root word. When you have entered all the words correctly, the words in the numbered groups will fit into the spaces in the answer below. One word has been entered into the grid for you as an example.

Answer to the Riddle:

One _____ his _____, and the other _____ his _____.
       1   2   3   4

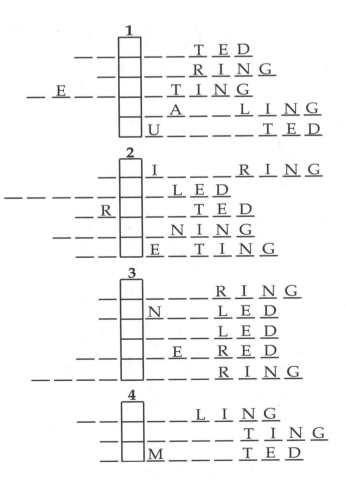

1
_ _ _ | | _ T E D
_ _ | | R I N G
_ E _ | | T I N G
_ _ | | A _ _ L I N G
_ | | U _ _ _ T E D

2
_ | | I _ _ R I N G
_ _ _ _ | | L E D
_ R _ | | T E D
_ _ _ | | N I N G
_ _ _ | | E _ T I N G

3
_ _ | | R I N G
_ | | N _ L E D
_ | | _ L E D
_ | | E _ R E D
_ _ _ _ | | R I N G

4
_ _ _ | | L I N G
_ _ | | T I N G
_ | | M _ _ _ T E D

Root Words	
cancel	rebel
✓commit	submit
control	total
defer	transfer
dispel	transmit
flicker	travel
permit	waver
prefer	upset
profit	whimper

Name_____ **Date** _____

Maze

Directions: Find the shortest path to the finish by passing through 25 correctly spelled words. You cannot pass through a solid line or an area containing a misspelled word. Be careful! Some paths lead to dead ends.

★ **Bonus:** How many correctly spelled words, including Start and Finish, are there in the entire maze? _____

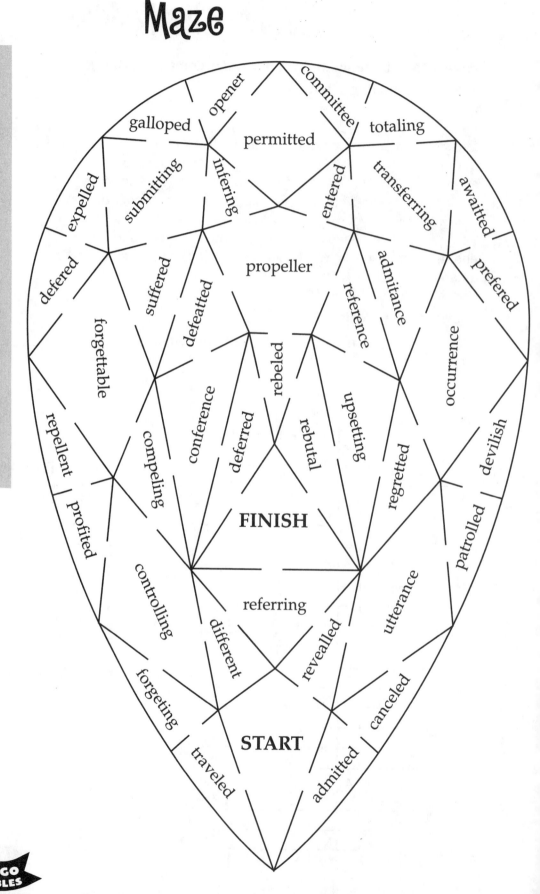

galloped
opener
committee
totaling
permitted
expelled
submitting
infering
entered
transferring
awaitted
defered
suffered
defeatted
propeller
admitance
reference
prefered
forgettable
rebeled
occurrence
conference
deferred
rebutal
upsetting
regretted
devilish
repellent
compeling
FINISH
utterance
patrolled
profited
controlling
referring
revealled
canceled
different
forgeting
traveled
START
admitted

Unit 7: The *i* Before *e* Rule

Br ie **f   r** ei **n   rec** ei **ve**

Unit 7 presents what is probably the first spelling rule we all learn as children, taught through one of the best-known rhymes in the English language. But being able to rattle off the rule doesn't always translate into correctly spelled *ie* and *ei* words. The lesson and exercises in this unit help students clarify and apply the rule accurately.

The *i* Before *e* Rule: Use *i* before *e* except after *c* or when sounded like /ā/ as in *neighbor* and *weigh*.

Teaching Tip

★ Often confusion occurs because students don't realize that the rhyme isn't quite complete. It should really say "**immediately** after *c*," not just "after *c*." Without that clarification, it might seem right, for example, to spell the word *chief* as *cheif*.

Exceptions to the rule:

1. The real problem for all of us is that there are so many instances of the *ie* pattern besides "after *c*" and "sounds like /ā/." There is, however, a nonsense sentence that can serve as a memory device for some of the most common exceptions:

Neither leisurely foreigner seized their weird height.

2. Words like *species* and *efficient* in which the *ci* makes the /sh/ sound.

3. Words like *science* and *society* in which there is a syllable break between the *i* and the *e*.

4. The word *sheik* if pronounced /shēk/ rather than /shāk/.

No exceptions (other than the ones in the rule itself—"after *c*" and "sounds like /ā/") are included in the exercises in this unit.

Mini-Lesson

This rule is so well known that students often "tune out" when it is taught again. New approaches are needed to stimulate interest and help students realize that they may never have internalized the meaning of the *i* before *e* rhyme.

Ask a few students to recite the *i* before *e* rhyme. Then ask a student to tell the class just two exceptions to the *i* before *e* combination that are mentioned in the rule itself. If your class is like most, that question will surprise and even stump many students. They haven't quite realized that most of the rhyme—all of it after the first four words!—teaches when to use *e* before *i*! In other words, they never really have separated in their minds *ie* words and *ei* words or identified the patterns that help us figure out which combination to use.

After going over the "after *c*" and "sounds like /ā/" exceptions, write three headings on the board—*ie*, *ei after c*, and *ei sounding like /ā/*. How many words can the class come up with on their own? Ask students to stick to words that fit the rule, even though there are exceptions. Then as a bonus (treated as a weird secret instead of a lesson, most students love to learn this) teach them the sentence of common exceptions: *Neither leisurely foreigner seized their weird height.*

Answers

Page 35, Solve the Riddle
Clues: 1. ceiling **2.** field **3.** sleigh **4.** niece
5. grief **6.** mischief **7.** receipt **8.** conceive
9. thief **10.** relief **11.** achievement
12. overweight **13.** chief **14.** friends
Answer to the riddle: He had more cents.

Page 36, Would You Vote for This Candidate?
1. neighbor **2.** brief **3.** beliefs **4.** grief
5. believe **6.** shrieking **7.** receive **8.** their
9. height **10.** ceiling **11.** relieved
12. mischievous **13.** conceive **14.** pieces
15. fiendish **16.** friends **17.** neighbors
18. weigh **19.** perceive

Page 37, Maze
The shortest path to the finish passes through: 1. relie, **2.** belief **3.** receipt
4. conceive **5.** relieve **6.** perceive **7.** freight **8.** achieve **9.** veil
Bonus: 19; all the above plus Start, Finish, friend, receive, handkerchief, neighbor, rein, niece, shriek, brief

Spelling Puzzles & Mazes • Scholastic Professional Books

Name_____ Date _____

Solve the Riddle

Riddle: A nickel and a dime were sitting on a dock. The nickel fell into the water. Why didn't the dime?

Answer: __ __   __ __ __   __ __ __ __   __ __ __ __ __.
       1 2   3 4 5   6 7 8 9   10 11 12 13 14

Directions: Fill in the blank spaces after the clues with the correctly spelled words. Copy the letters from the numbered lines into the matching answer spaces to reveal the answer to the riddle. The words for all the answers to the clues appear in the box below, but with blanks where they have an *ie* or *ei* combination. You will have to add these letters in order to fit them into the spaces correctly.

ach_ _vement	c_ _ling	ch_ _f	conc_ _ve	f_ _ld	fr_ _nds	gr_ _f
misch_ _f	n_ _ce	rec_ _pt	rel_ _f	sl_ _gh	th_ _f	overw_ _ght

Clues

1. The part of the room over your head is the __ __ __ __ __ __ __.
          10

2. Football is often played on a grassy __ __ __ __ __.
          5

3. A carriage that goes over snow is a __ __ __ __ __ __.
       14

4. The daughter of a woman's brother is her __ __ __ __ __.
         2

5. The feeling you get when a loved one dies is __ __ __ __ __.
        8

6. Another word for naughty behavior is __ __ __ __ __ __ __ __.
       6

7. A paper proving you bought something is a __ __ __ __ __ __ __.
          13

8. When you can't imagine something, you can't __ __ __ __ __ __ __ __ it.
         9

9. A person who steals is a __ __ __ __ __.
     1

10. After a hard job, you can breathe a sigh of __ __ __ __ __ __.
         11

11. Something well done is an __ __ __ __ __ __ __ __ __ __ __.
      4

12. Another word for extreme *heaviness* is __ __ __ __ __ __ __ __ __.
      7

13. One of the U.S. president's titles is commander in __ __ __ __ __.
      3

14. People who like each other are __ __ __ __ __ __ __.
      12

Name_____ Date _____

Would You Vote for This Candidate?

There was going to be an election for class president at the Wildwood School. Tomas Perez was one of the candidates, and this was one of his campaign speeches.

Directions: In this copy of Tomas's speech there are decisions to make about the spelling of words that contain the *ie* or *ei* letter combinations. For each pair of choices, underline the correct form. The first one has been done for you.

Hint: The speech contains two words that are exceptions to the rule.

Like my opponent, my (nieghbor, <u>neighbor</u>) Amanda Meyers, I have been asked to give a (brief , breif) account of my goals and (beliefs, beleifs) so that you can decide if you want me as your next class president. I also want to give my opinion about some of my opponent's ideas, which I think will lead us into trouble and (grief, greif). Okay, here goes.

First, I (believe, beleive) that there are not enough grades given at Wildwood. I hear you moaning and even (shrieking, shreiking), but let me finish. I think that the teachers should get grades, too. Yes, if they give, then they should (recieve, receive), too! We could give them grades on homework assignments, on test fairness, and on the quality of (thier, their) jokes. Well, maybe not the jokes—we don't want to flunk them all out!

Second, unlike my opponent, Amanda, who wants to raise the (hieght, height) of the (cieling, ceiling) in the gym, I think we should leave it where it is. Okay, so fifteen feet is a little low, but think how many games we win because the other teams don't know how to bank the ball off the roof!

Third, you will be (releived, relieved) to hear that, unlike my opponent, I do not support the school board's (mischievous, mischeivous) new policy of replacing the old school buses with new ones. No, I think they should replace all the buses with stretch limousines! Can you (concieve, conceive) it? No more bouncing around on those hard seats. No more (peices, pieces) of chewing gum stuck in our hair by that (feindish, fiendish) kid in the seat behind us. And a TV in every limo to entertain us as we purr down the road!

So, my (friends, freinds), (neighbors, nieghbors), and fellow students, I ask you to think about my ideas and (wiegh, weigh) them against those of my opponent. I think you'll quickly (percieve, perceive) that I am the one that you should vote for.

Spelling Puzzles & Mazes • Scholastic Professional Books

Maze

Directions: Find the shortest path to the finish by passing through nine correctly spelled words. You cannot pass through a solid line or an area containing a misspelled word. Be careful! Some paths lead to dead ends.

★ **Bonus:** How many correctly spelled words, including Start and Finish, are there in the entire maze? _____

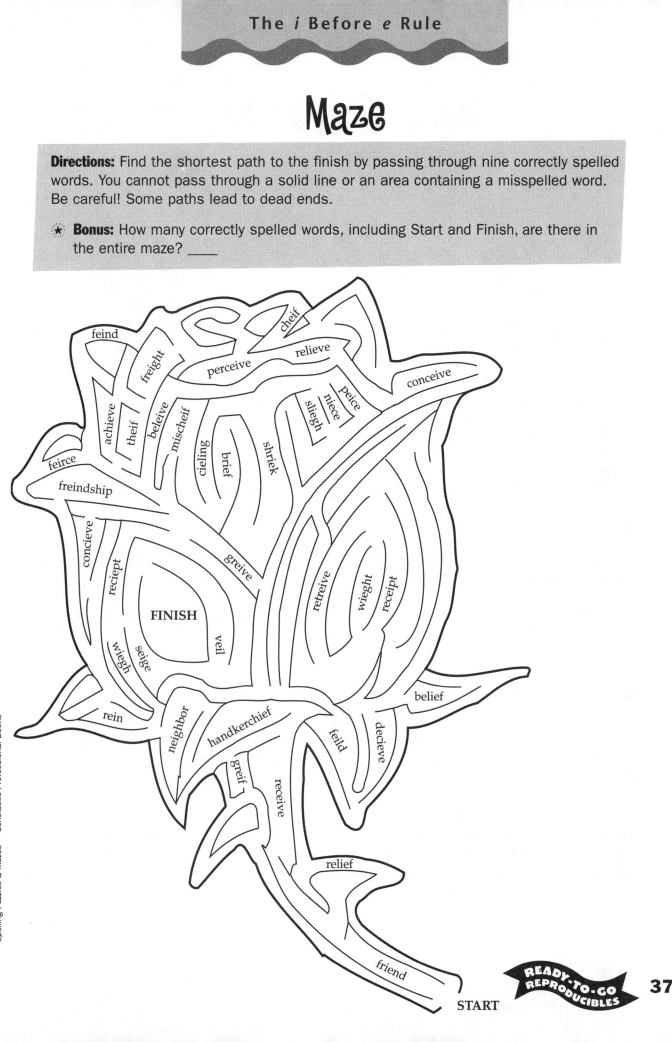

Unit 8: Contractions

Unit 8 provides practice for the correct placement of apostrophes according to the general rule for contractions.

Rule: The apostrophe is placed where the letters of one word have been omitted, not where the two words are joined.

Teaching Tip

★ Contractions are usually misspelled in one of two ways: the apostrophe is omitted or is inserted in the wrong spot. In a few cases, misspellings arise from using too many letters (*I'ld*) or from misspelling one of the combining words (*dosen't*).

Mini-Lesson

Since students often neglect to use the apostrophe when writing contractions, it is a good idea to show them just why they are needed. Better still, it is a good idea to let them discover this reason for themselves.

Spelling Puzzles & Mazes • Scholastic Professional Books

Write the words *should not* on the board and ask a volunteer to explain how to write the contraction. Surely, many students will know that it's *shouldn't*. Ask why we need the apostrophe at all—why not write *shouldnt*? Someone may offer the answer that we need the apostrophe to show that a letter has been omitted—an excellent observation that should be commended.

But then pursue the topic: Wouldn't we understand perfectly if the apostrophe wasn't there? Are there times when we really need that apostrophe to avoid confusion? If you're lucky, you will find a couple of excited students who realize that without the apostrophe, words like *I'll*, *we'll*, *we'd*, and *she'd* could easily be confused with *ill*, *well*, *wed*, and *shed*. We need to *see* that letters have been omitted in order to avoid misreading—not to mention the fact that *wouldnt*, *shes*, and *whos* look very funny!

Answers

Page 40, Maze
The correct path goes through:
1. shouldn't (Slow Town) **2.** isn't (Beachville) **3.** couldn't (Plains City)
4. there's (State Park) **5.** let's (Twin City) **6.** we've (Ocean Beach)

Page 41, What Is My Name?
1. they're **2.** can't **3.** don't **4.** didn't **5.** she'd **6.** couldn't **7.** isn't **8.** I've
9. where's **10.** I'm **11.** wouldn't
Grid answers: wolverine, MI (Michigan)

Name_____ **Date** _____

Maze

Directions: Trace a path to Ocean Beach through six correctly spelled contractions. You cannot pass through any areas with misspelled contractions; they act like blocks and force you to go back and try a different route.

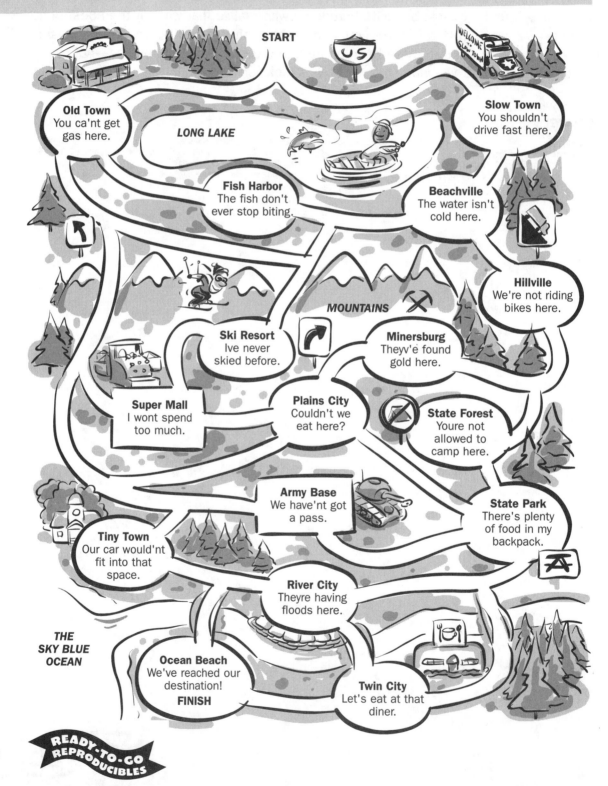

START

Old Town
You ca'nt get gas here.

LONG LAKE

Slow Town
You shouldn't drive fast here.

Fish Harbor
The fish don't ever stop biting.

Beachville
The water isn't cold here.

Hillville
We're not riding bikes here.

MOUNTAINS

Ski Resort
Ive never skied before.

Minersburg
Theyv'e found gold here.

Super Mall
I wont spend too much.

Plains City
Couldn't we eat here?

State Forest
Youre not allowed to camp here.

Army Base
We have'nt got a pass.

State Park
There's plenty of food in my backpack.

Tiny Town
Our car would'nt fit into that space.

River City
Theyre having floods here.

THE SKY BLUE OCEAN

Ocean Beach
We've reached our destination!
FINISH

Twin City
Let's eat at that diner.

READY-TO-GO REPRODUCIBLES

Spelling Puzzles & Mazes • Scholastic Professional Books

Name _____ **Date** _____

What Is My Name?

I'm a carnivorous animal with a bushy tail. The people
of one state chose me for their state nickname. I'm a _____

Directions: To spell out the name of the animal and the abbreviation of the state's name, first fill in the missing contractions in the clues. Then transfer the words into the grid below. Be careful to match the number of the sentence with the number along the grid.

Hints: The word combinations that make up the correct contractions appear in the box below. Be sure to put the apostrophes (') in the right places when you write the contractions! Use each combination only once.

can not	could not	did not	do not	I am	I have	is not	she had	they are	where is	would not

1. The kids have been dancing six hours, and

now __ __ __ __ __ __ feeling a little tired.

2. I can sing well, but I __ __ __ __ whistle through my teeth.

3. If you aren't a fish or a robin, then you probably __ __ __ __ like worms.

4. We liked Barry's new blue sneakers, but we __ __ __ __ __ care for his orange jeans.

5. Sheila's dress was all dirty because __ __ __ __ forgotten to bring her football uniform.

6. We tried, but even with a telescope we __ __ __ __ __ __ __ see any chocolate on Mars.

7. There __ __ __ __ enough ketchup on my peanut butter sandwich!

8. I know that flying squirrels exist, but __ __ __ never seen one at the airport.

9. The jobless wizard asked the dentist, "__ __ __ __ __ __ my wisdom tooth?"

10. "__ __ so happy that we went to the circus!" said Carmella to Sylvester, her pet elephant.

11. Most people __ __ __ __ __ __ __ enjoy a swim in the Arctic Ocean in December.

11. ☐ __ __ __ __ __ __
3. __☐__ __
6. __ __☐__ __ __
8. __☐__ __
1. __ __☐__ __
9. __ __ __☐__ __
7. __☐__
2. __ __☐__
5. __ __☐__
10. __☐
4. __☐__

Spelling Puzzles & Mazes • Scholastic Professional Books

Unit 9: Plurals and Singular Possessives

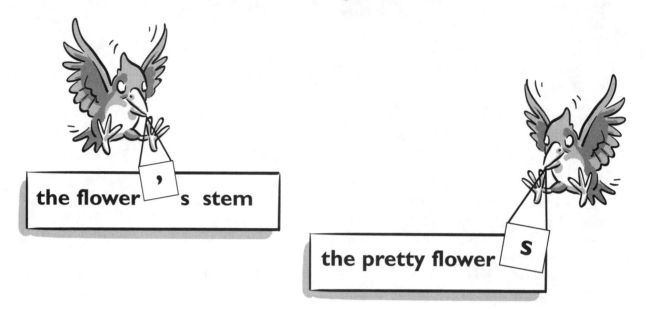

the flower's stem

the pretty flower s

Units 9 and 10 address the confusion caused by the use of final -s in forming both plurals and possessives. What's the reason for this spelling confusion? On the historical road to modern English we adopted Romance languages' use of final -s for the formation of plurals. Unluckily, we also borrowed the Germanic languages' use of final -s for the formation of possessives. Since we were saddled with identical sounds used for different purposes, the apostrophe was inserted in written English to signal a possessive rather than a plural, but it is very hard for students—for all of us!—to remember to use these apostrophes and to use them correctly.

This unit focuses on differentiating between plurals and singular possessives. Because they hear no difference between *flowers* and *flower's*, students often forget to use the apostrophe in expressions like *the flower's stem*. Sometimes the mistake is reversed: an apostrophe is used incorrectly to make a plural—*the pretty flower's*.

Rule: To make a singular possessive, write the singular word and add -'s.

Teaching Tip

Exception to the rule:
The possessives of words that are singular and already end in -s or -es are sometimes written by adding only an apostrophe rather than -'s, especially if the extra syllable is not pronounced—*Massachusetts' streets are very clean*. It is usually preferable and never incorrect, however, to add the -'s—*Massachusetts's streets are very clean*.

Spelling Puzzles & Mazes • Scholastic Professional Books

Mini-Lesson

Students are more likely to remember to use apostrophes—and to use them correctly—if they understand why they are needed. To help them see this, write a sentence on the board, like *The storm damaged the trees flowers and leaves*, telling the class that you have purposely omitted all punctuation. Ask individual students what the sentence means to them. You will surely get different interpretations, all of them correct since no commas or apostrophes were provided:

The storm damaged three things: trees, flowers, and leaves.

The storm damaged one tree's flowers and leaves.

The storm damaged many trees' flowers and leaves.

Explain that it was to prevent just this kind of ambiguity that apostrophes were introduced, and then write the sentence three ways, each with punctuation and spelling that correctly represents its meaning.

Before going on to the written exercises, do a quick oral drill. Ask the class to decide if the "s word" in each sentence that you read is a plural or a singular possessive. Try sentences like *I gave her some flowers* and *This flower's petals are falling off*. Inform your students that they aren't going to have to worry about plural possessives today—and they will probably be very relieved!

Answers

Page 44, Hidden Message
Correctly spelled words: 1. squirrel's, nuts **2.** cones **3.** magician's, doves **4.** streets, balloons **5.** Megan's, father's **6.** pitcher's, balls, catcher's **7.** sneakers, socks **8.** rainbow's, city's **9.** sisters, snake's **10.** tiger's, stripes, lights **11.** butterfly's, wings **12.** inches, girl's, dresses **13.** soldier's, eyes
Message: dog

Page 45, Maze
The shortest path to the exit goes through: 1. That zebra's stripes are amazing! **2.** Who feeds these giraffes? **3.** The walrus's pool is dirty. **4.** What is the gorilla's name? **5.** The sea lions all love fish. **6.** That buffalo's head is huge. **7.** The monkeys are funny. **8.** The parrots are so noisy. **9.** The coyotes look like dogs. **10.** The elephant's trunk is so long! **11.** The panda's eyes look sweet and kind. **12.** Do you think that the skunks can still spray? **13.** The wolf cub's mother is very patient with him. **14.** The jackrabbits have very long ears and legs. **15.** That rhinoceros's hide looks very thick and tough.

Name_____ **Date** _____

Hidden Message

Cheryl has just noticed that something large is in her bed. But if she could read the secret message in her patchwork quilt, she wouldn't be afraid to turn back the covers. She would know that it was only her _____.

Directions: To figure out the message in the quilt, circle only the correctly spelled words in the following sentences. Shade in the grid squares that match the number-letter pairs above the correctly spelled words you've circled. The first one has been done for you.

Clues

1. The (squirrels, **squirrel's**) nest was full of (nuts, nut's).
   [K–2] [N–9] [E–1] [A–5]

2. "I scream when I see icy ice cream (cones, cone's)," Tai screamed.
   [H–4] [F–8]

3. The (magicians, magician's) magical cape made the three white (doves, dove's) disappear.
   [M–4] [M–9] [B–3] [C–7]

4. Over the (streets, street's) of the city hovered six bright red (balloons, balloon's).
   [G–6] [N–3] [N–7] [H–1]

5. When (Megans, Megan's) fever rose, her (fathers, father's) concern rose with it.
   [D–4] [C–1] [J–5] [L–7]

6. The (pitchers, pitcher's) fast (balls, ball's) hurt the (catchers, catcher's) hand.
   [A–9] [J–8] [E–3] [G–3] [I–2] [I–5]

7. Lateef liked his (sneakers, sneaker's) dirty but his (socks, sock's) clean.
   [L–8] [M–1] [C–2] [D–5]

8. The (rainbows, rainbow's) end rested on the top of the (cities, city's) highest skyscraper.
   [L–5] [F–5] [H–9] [A–3]

9. The three (sisters, sister's) seemed surprised that the (snakes, snake's) skin was soft and dry.
   [J–9] [B–6] [N–4] [G–4]

10. One (tigers, tiger's) (stripes, stripe's) seemed to glow in the dark like black and orange
    [A–1] [J–7] [E–2] [M–6]
    neon (lights, light's).
    [L–9] [A–4]

11. The newly hatched (butterflies, butterfly's) (wings, wing's) were still wet.
    [E–6] [K–7] [D–1] [D–8]

12. Since she had grown two (inches, inch's) over the summer, the little (girls, girl's)
    [N–8] [J–4] [N–2] [D–3]
    old (dresses, dress's) no longer fit her.
    [H–6] [A–7]

13. The old (soldiers, soldier's) face was wrinkled, but his (eyes, eye's) were young and bright.
    [G–7] [C–3] [K–9] [J–1]

Spelling Puzzles & Mazes • Scholastic Professional Books

Name_____ Date _____

Maze

Directions: The school bus is leaving students at the entrance to the zoo and will pick them up later at the exit. Help guide the students to the exit by following the shortest path that leads through 15 sentences containing only correctly spelled words. If a sentence contains a word that is misspelled, stop and go back. You cannot pass through a solid line or an area containing a misspelling.

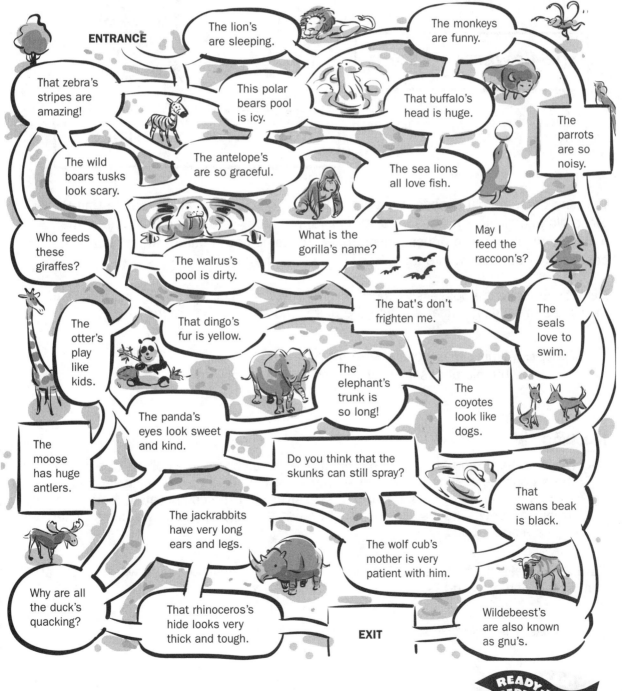

ENTRANCE

The lion's are sleeping.

The monkeys are funny.

That zebra's stripes are amazing!

This polar bears pool is icy.

That buffalo's head is huge.

The parrots are so noisy.

The wild boars tusks look scary.

The antelope's are so graceful.

The sea lions all love fish.

Who feeds these giraffes?

The walrus's pool is dirty.

What is the gorilla's name?

May I feed the raccoon's?

The bat's don't frighten me.

The seals love to swim.

The otter's play like kids.

That dingo's fur is yellow.

The elephant's trunk is so long!

The coyotes look like dogs.

The moose has huge antlers.

The panda's eyes look sweet and kind.

Do you think that the skunks can still spray?

That swans beak is black.

The jackrabbits have very long ears and legs.

The wolf cub's mother is very patient with him.

Why are all the duck's quacking?

That rhinoceros's hide looks very thick and tough.

EXIT

Wildebeest's are also known as gnu's.

Unit 10: Plurals, Singular Possessives, and Plural Possessives

the flowers' stem

the children's smiles

This unit presents plural possessives, building on the concepts addressed in Unit 9. Since plurals, singular possessives, and plural possessives all sound the same, the already difficult problem of using apostrophes becomes even harder when plural possessives are thrown into the mix.

Rule 1: To make the possessive form of a word with a regular plural (nouns that form their plural by adding a final -s), write the plural and add an apostrophe after it.

> **Example:** All his *shirts'* collars were frayed.
> (The plural of *shirt* is *shirts* and the possessive plural is *shirts'*.)

Teaching Tip

★ Most of the exercises in this unit ask students to choose the correct one of the three possible -s endings for nouns—the -s for plurals, the -'s for singular possessives, and the -s' for regular plural possessives. But the complicating factor of irregular plurals—nouns like *child* that do not form their plurals by adding a final -s—is also included.

Rule 2: To make the possessive form of a word with an irregular plural, write the plural form of the word and add -'s.

> **Example:** The *children's* shirts were dirty.

Spelling Puzzles & Mazes • Scholastic Professional Books

Mini-Lesson

Reintroduce students to the example sentence from the Unit 9 Mini-Lesson: *The storm damaged the trees flowers and leaves*. Again omit all punctuation. Review the three possible interpretations of those words:

The storm damaged three things: trees, flowers, and leaves.

The storm damaged one tree's flowers and leaves.

The storm damaged many trees' flowers and leaves.

This time stress that without some way to differentiate between singular and plural possessives, we could not know whether the writer meant that the flowers and leaves of one tree sustained damage or that many trees were affected. Then write three correct sentences that each represent one of the above meanings.

Next, let students try placing apostrophes in the correct place orally. Add plurals, too, so that the students have to figure out which of the three forms you are using. Try sentences like *This dog's collar is too loose*, *The two dogs' toys are lost*, and *Dogs are lucky that they never have to learn how to spell!*

Answers

Page 48, What's Wrong With This Picture?
Plurals that should end in -s:
goblins, Bags, powers, stains, displays
Singular possessives that should end in -'s:
cat's, sorcerer's, moon's, coffin's, Dracula's, father's
Plural possessives that should end in -s':
witches', ladies', cats', werewolves', snakes'

Page 49, Maze
The shortest route to the end passes through: 1. I like **Julia's** new haircut. **2.** Are these **boards** too short? **3.** The **jar's** lid is very loose. **4.** The two **eagles'** nest was huge. **5.** This **store's windows** are dirty. **6.** These **deer's antlers** all have eight **points. 7.** I love your pearl **earrings. 8.** The **knife's** edge is razor sharp. **9.** We saw six **boys' bicycles. 10.** How many **legs** do **flies** have? **11.** These **pencils' erasers** don't work. **12.** This **road's curves** are annoying. **13.** My **trousers' pockets** are torn. **14.** The **Earth's oceans** are vast. **15.** I found the **puzzle's** solution.

Page 50, Alliteration Puzzle
Misspelled words: 1. sculptors' **2.** mother's, pies **3.** history's **4.** cousins' **5.** noodles **6.** firefighters' **7.** Grandma's **8.** towels, train's **9.** barriers, bandits **10.** children's, Carol's
Puzzle key: THIS (bandits, firefighters', children's, pies); WAS (towels, train's, Carol's); NOT (cousins', sculptors', mother's); EASY (noodles, Grandma's, barriers, history's)
Message: This was not easy.

Name_____ Date _____

What's Wrong With This Picture?

Directions: The Halloween Museum may be full of visual treats, but it seems to play tricks on some of the people who work and visit there. It makes them misuse apostrophes. See if you can you find 16 spelling errors that they have made. Write the misspelled words correctly in the appropriate spaces.

Spelling Corrections

Plurals that should end in -**s**:	Singular possessives that should end in -**'s**:	Plural possessives that should end in -**s'**:
1. _____	1. _____	1. _____
2. _____	2. _____	2. _____
3. _____	3. _____	3. _____
4. _____	4. _____	4. _____
5. _____	5. _____	5. _____
	6. _____	

These witches broom-sticks are supersonic!

This black cats tail has magical powers'.

These goblin's are friendly.

The werewolves love the full moons light.

Please don't touch the display's or feed the vampire bats!

All the cats eyes look evil!

Those three old lady's fingernails need cleaning!

That werewolf's howl sounds like your fathers voice when he sings.

The werewolves howls give me goosebumps!

Draculas eyes just opened!

Beware! These bats' fangs may scare you!

The coffins lid has bloodstain's!

Yuk! The cauldron is full of snake's tails and toadstools.

Record-Breaking Trick-or-Treat Bag's

Do not drink from this sorcerers cauldron!

This gentleman's bed is a coffin!

READY-TO-GO REPRODUCIBLES

Name_____ **Date** _____

Maze

Directions: Find the path to the end by passing only through spaces containing words in **bold** that are correctly spelled. The shortest path will take you through 15 spaces with correct spellings.

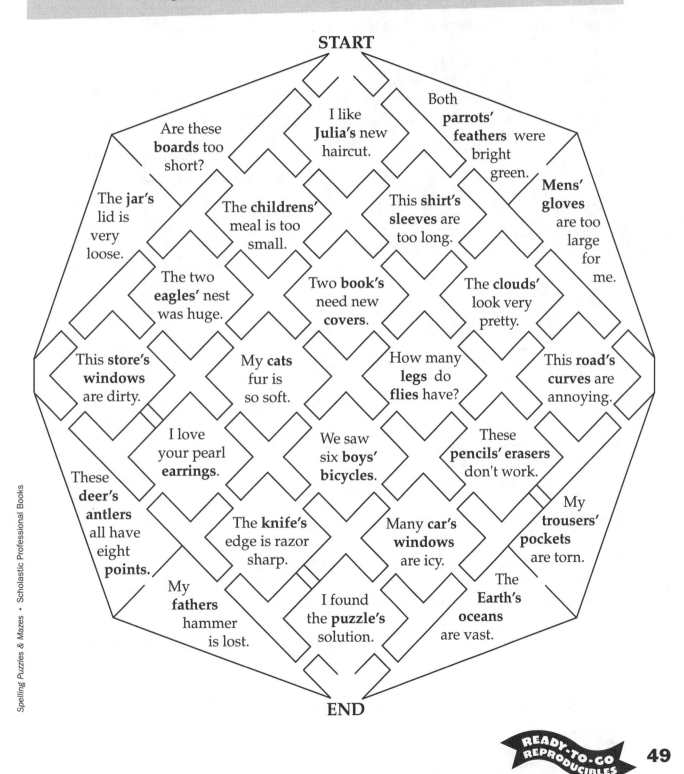

START

Are these **boards** too short?

I like **Julia's** new haircut.

Both **parrots' feathers** were bright green.

Mens' gloves are too large for me.

The **jar's** lid is very loose.

The **childrens'** meal is too small.

This **shirt's sleeves** are too long.

The two **eagles'** nest was huge.

Two **book's** need new **covers**.

The **clouds'** look very pretty.

This **store's windows** are dirty.

My **cats** fur is so soft.

How many **legs** do **flies** have?

This **road's curves** are annoying.

I love your pearl **earrings**.

We saw six **boys' bicycles**.

These **pencils' erasers** don't work.

These **deer's antlers** all have eight **points**.

The **knife's** edge is razor sharp.

Many **car's windows** are icy.

My **trousers' pockets** are torn.

My **fathers** hammer is lost.

I found the **puzzle's** solution.

The **Earth's oceans** are vast.

END

READY-TO-GO REPRODUCIBLES

Name_____ **Date** _____

Alliteration Puzzle

Directions: The sentences below are full of alliteration—the repetition of beginning consonant sounds—and they are also full of misspelled plurals and possessives. Find the 14 misspelled words and underline them. Then write the correct spellings so that each word fits exactly on one line of the grid. When you are finished, the vertical boxes will spell out a message. One example has been done for you.

Hint: Use the letters and apostrophes in the grid to help you fill in the grid spaces with the correct answers.

```
_ _ n _ _ _ [ ] s
_ _ _ _ _ _ _ _ _ _ [ ] _ _ _ s '
_ _ _ _ [ ] _ _ _ _ ' s
_ _ _ [s]

_ _ _ [ ] _ s
_ _ _ [ ] i ' s
_ r _ _ ' [s]

_ _ _ s _ [ ] s '
s c u l p t [o] r s '
_ o [ ] _ _ _ _ ' s

_ _ o _ _ [ ] s
_ _ _ [ ] n _ _ _ ' s
_ _ _ _ _ [s]
_ _ s _ [ ] ' s
```

1. Six <u>sculptors</u> sculptures were scattered helter-skelter across the seashore.

2. My mothers mother makes masterful music and memorable mince pie's.

3. His hard-hearted helpers hummed happily when hearing of histories heartbreaks.

4. My two cousin's cute cats create constant craziness.

5. There are no noodle's on Nancy's newest menu.

6. Five firefighter's fire trucks faced the fiery inferno.

7. I guess Grandmas gas guzzler is still going great guns.

8. Who thoughtlessly tossed those two tattered towel's from the trains top?

9. Those big bank buildings have barriers' before them as barricades against battering bandit's.

10. The childrens' crying caused Carols canaries to kick and curse.

Unit 11: Homophone Demons

The [two] birds were [too] happy [to] stop singing at dark.

This unit deals with some of the most frequently misspelled words in the English language, yet they're not words that appear on "spelling demons" lists. In fact, they are very common words that we use in almost every conversation, but since they are all confusing *homophones* or *homonyms* (words that sound alike but are spelled differently), they cause chronic spelling problems. There is probably not a single writer of English who has not at some time inadvertently misspelled one of these words:

    its–it's   there–their–they're   whose–who's   your–you're   to–too–two

Rule: Possessive pronouns are already possessive and need no apostrophe.

Teaching Tips

☀ Notice that, except for the last group (*to, too,* and *two*), one of the words in each set of homophones is a possessive pronoun and one is a contraction. Since we use apostrophes to make *nouns* possessive, many students get confused and use an apostrophe when writing possessive pronouns—*The dog has lost **it's*** (instead of ***its***) *bone.*

☀ Remind students that just as they shouldn't write *his* as *hi's*, neither should they write *its* as *it's* or *your* as *you're* if they mean to use the possessive form.

Even if students know that the possessive form is *its* without the apostrophe, they still sometimes have problems knowing if they need a possessive or a contraction. There is an easy test to solve this problem: Substitute the uncontracted two words for the problem word and see if the sentence makes sense:

Problem:	The dog lost (its, it's) bone.
Test:	The dog lost *it is* bone?
Solution:	No, *it is* doesn't make sense, so the contraction is not correct; use *its*.

Problem:	I think (your, you're) right.
Test:	I think *you are* right?
Solution:	Yes, *you are* makes sense, so use the contraction form, *you're*.

Mini-Lesson

Tell the class that you are about to write a word on the board that just might be the most frequently misspelled word in the English language—and it only has three letters. If no one comes up with it, write *its* on the board. Ask why that little word is so often misspelled, and even if no one guessed it the first time, surely now someone will say that it is so often confused with *it's*.

Let this discussion lead into a brief discussion of homophones and then of the material outlined in Teaching Tips above: (1) possessive pronouns need no apostrophes (you wouldn't write *hi's*); and (2) the substitution test will tell whether a contraction or a possessive is needed.

Put up the above list of homophone groups and see if anyone in the class has a memory device to help distinguish among *to, too,* and *two*. Finally, ask the students if they can come up with sentences in which they use all the words in one homophone group in a single sentence—*They're practicing for their game over there by the gym*. Try to get a sentence or two for each of the five groups, making sure, perhaps by having the students write their sentences on the board, that the words are spelled correctly.

Answers

Page 53, What Is the Moral of This Story?
Correctly spelled words: (a) It's, too
(b) There's, to, your **(c)** Who's, their
(d) Two, their **(e)** Whose, there **(f)** too, their
(g) It's, whose, it's
Moral: It may take **two tries** to achieve **true ties.**

Page 54, Hidden Message
Correctly spelled words: 1. two, to **2.** There's, your, it's, to (E14), your **3.** Whose **4.** their, they're **5.** There's, It's, too, their (E15) **6.** who's, it's (C4) **7.** Your **8.** theirs, its (B9) **9.** whose, It's, to (C8) **10.** you're (C16) **11.** There's, its (D14), to **12.** you're, too (D10), there's, to.
The thief: crow

Page 55, Maze
The shortest route to the end passes through: 1. I wonder **who's** going to be the lead in the school play. **2. It's** often hard for me to sing a solo. **3.** Is this our group's report or **theirs? 4.** I missed **two** words on the spelling quiz. **5.** More problems? Good. I think **they're** fun! **6.** Are these **your** books? **7. There's** no more chalk. **8.** Some students forgot **their** notebooks. **9.** We've got **too** much homework tonight. **10. Whose** pen is this? **11.** The computer has a problem with **its** printer. **12.** I think **your** bus just left without you!

Spelling Puzzles & Mazes • Scholastic Professional Books

Name_____ **Date** _____

What Is the Moral of This Story?

Marty and Stacy went to the midway at the State Fair to see if they could win a prize in one of the games. They were immediately drawn to a barker who was calling, "Knock down all the bottles with one ball and you win an authentic, hand-painted silk tie!"

"I'm going to win a tie for you!" Stacy said to Marty.

She gave the attendant a dollar, took a ball, threw it— and missed the pyramid of bottles entirely.

"That's okay," said Marty. "I'm a good baseball player and I couldn't make a perfect pitch either."

But Stacy wanted to try again.

"Really," said Marty, "save your money. We'll find an easier game."

"You'll see," said Stacy. She handed the attendant another dollar and picked up another ball.

Taking a deep breath, she concentrated, reared back, and threw again. The ball caught the outside of the bottle in the left-hand corner of the bottom row, and that bottle fell sideways into the one next to it, creating a chain reaction that brought the whole pyramid down.

"That's the perfect shot!" exclaimed the attendant, and he was so impressed that he handed Stacy two silk ties.

She gave the two ties to Marty, who was so proud of her that he asked her to marry him. Two years later they had a big wedding, and they lived very happily together for many, many years.

Moral: It may take __ __ __   *t* __ __ __ __ to achieve __ __ __ __   __ __ __ __.
         1 2 3   4 5 6 7 8   9 10 11 12   13 14 15 16

Directions: To discover the moral, find the correctly spelled words in each sentence below. There is one letter in each correctly spelled word that is underlined with a number under it. Write that letter in the matching answer space. The first one has been done for you.

(a) (It's, Its) (to, too) windy for us to go on the Ferris wheel today.
        4   1   10   3

(b) (Theirs, There's) no reason for you (to, too, two) worry about
         11   15   9   16   15

(your, you're) safety on the bumper cars.
 11   8

(c) (Whose, Who's) going with me on (their, there) little roller coaster?
         1   8   13   6

(d) (To, Two, Too) of (they're, their) rides are closed for repairs.
         2   2   9   16   10

(e) (Whose, Who's) ticket is lying (there, their) on the ground?
         7   1   5   14

(f) I'm (to, too, two) full for one of (they're, their, there) delicious hot dogs.
         10   1   13   15   6   3

(g) (It's, Its) still early, I think, but Daniel's father, (who's, whose) watch
         16   5   9   12

is always right, is saying that (its, it's) time to go home.
                                 1   14

Name_____ **Date** _____

Hidden Message

Ariel Mendoza's gold ring is missing! She was playing with her neighbors in their backyard, and when they decided to do gymnastics, she took her ring off so that it wouldn't get scratched. Ariel knows exactly where she put it—on the stump by the brick wall. But now it is gone, and no one can figure out who took it. . . . No one, that is, except you!

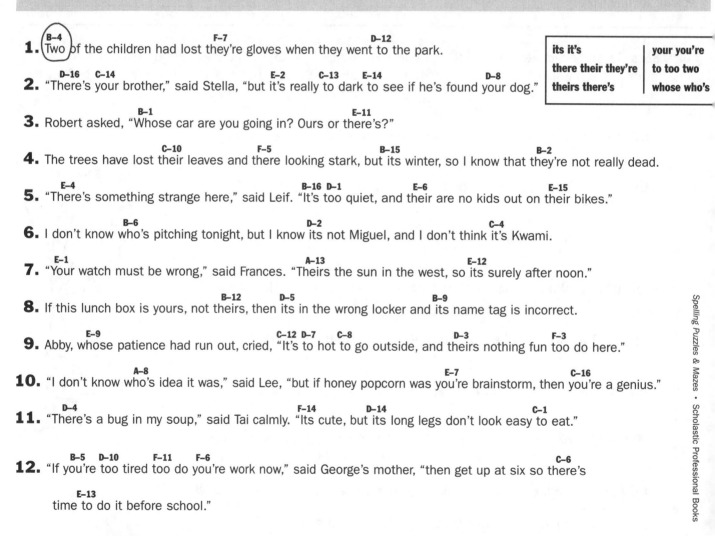

Directions: Circle only the correctly spelled homophone demons in the sentences below. Then go to the wall grid and shade in each brick that matches the number-letter pair written above the words you've circled. The name of the thief will appear. The first one has been done for you.

its it's	your you're
there their they're	to too two
theirs there's	whose who's

1. (**B–4** Two) of the children had lost **F–7** they're gloves when they went to the park. **D–12**

2. **D–16 C–14** "There's your brother," said Stella, "but it's really **E–2** to dark to see if he's **C–13 E–14** found your dog." **D–8**

3. Robert asked, "Whose car are you going in? **B–1** Ours or there's?" **E–11**

4. The trees have lost their leaves and **C–10** there looking stark, **F–5** but its winter, **B–15** so I know that they're not really dead. **B–2**

5. **E–4** "There's something strange here," said Leif. "It's too quiet, **B–16 D–1** and their are no kids out on their bikes." **E–6** **E–15**

6. I don't know **B–6** who's pitching tonight, but I know **D–2** its not Miguel, and I don't think **C–4** it's Kwami.

7. **E–1** "Your watch must be wrong," said Frances. "Theirs the sun in the west, **A–13** so its surely after noon." **E–12**

8. If this lunch box is yours, **B–12** not theirs, then **D–5** its in the wrong locker and **B–9** its name tag is incorrect.

9. **E–9** Abby, whose patience had run out, cried, "It's **C–12 D–7** to hot **C–8** to go outside, and theirs **D–3** nothing fun too do here." **F–3**

10. "I don't know **A–8** who's idea it was," said Lee, "but if honey popcorn was **E–7** you're brainstorm, then **C–16** you're a genius."

11. "There's **D–4** a bug in my soup," said Tai calmly. "Its cute, **F–14** but its **D–14** long legs don't look easy **C–1** to eat."

12. "If you're **B–5 D–10** too tired **F–11** too do **F–6** you're work now," said George's mother, "then get up at six so there's **C–6**

E–13 time to do it before school."

Spelling Puzzles & Mazes • Scholastic Professional Books

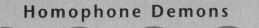

Name_____ Date _____

Maze

Miranda stayed late after basketball practice to shoot free throws, and then she left in such a hurry that she forgot her backpack in the locker room. By the time she had gone back and found it, everyone had left the school, and many of the doors were locked.

Directions: Help her find the way out of the school by avoiding all spelling errors. You may pass through only open doors and rooms in which the words in **bold** are spelled correctly. The shortest path will take you through 12 rooms containing correct spellings.

SCHOOL FLOOR PLAN

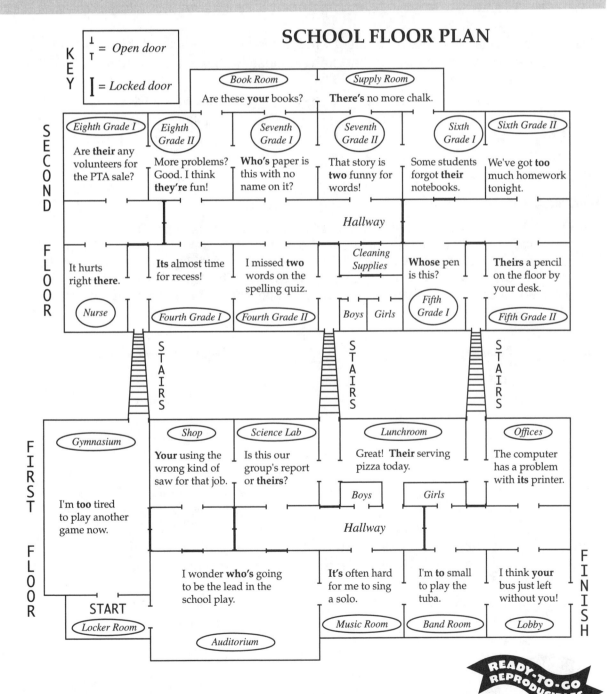

Unit 12: Similar Words

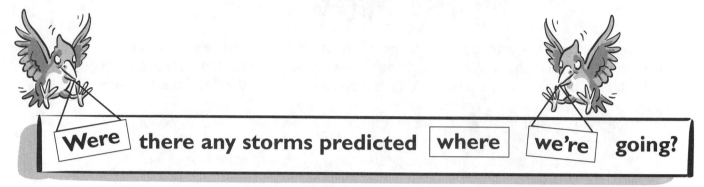

Were there any storms predicted **where** **we're** going?

This unit deals with nine sets of frequently misspelled words, some of them pairs of homophones, some of them words that are very close but not quite the same in spelling.

brake	break	coarse	course	lets	let's	
lose	loose	peace	piece	quiet	quite	
than	then	threw	through	were	we're	where

Teaching Tip

★ There is no easy way to help students learn which word is which in these pairs, but mnemonic devices often help. The best mnemonic device is one that you make up for yourself, a memory prompt that has personal meaning. Often, the sillier the prompt, the better it sticks in students' memories. The following list provides common meanings of each word in the pair and, for some, a mnemonic device that might be of help.

Word	Meaning	Mnemonic Device
brake	to slow down; stopping device	
break	snap; recess	"Eak! I broke it!"
coarse	*adj.* rough; vulgar	An *a* in the adjective form
course	*n.* school class; race track; "of course"	
lets	*3rd person singular verb* allows	Test using *let us* for *lets*:
let's	contraction: *let us*	If it works, it should be *let's.*
lose	*v.* to misplace; be defeated	"Did you lose an *o*?"
loose	*adj.* not tight; free; *v.* release	As loose as a moose
peace	rest; harmony	An *a* in war and peace
piece	part; segment	A *piece* of *pie*

Spelling Puzzles & Mazes • Scholastic Professional Books

Word	Meaning	Mnemonic Device
quiet	silent; still	Overpronounce: "Qui-et!"
quite	very; very much	
than	comparison word	An *a* in *as* and *than*
then	at that time; therefore	An *e* in *then* and *time*
threw	*v.* past tense of *throw*	We threw a few new pews.
through	*prep.* by way of, etc.	Go through rough dough.
were	past tense of verb *to be*	For *were* and *we're*, test
we're	contraction of *we are*	by using *we are*.
where	at or in what place	Aspirate the *h* heavily.

Mini-Lesson

Give each student in the class a list of the words above with their meanings but with blank spaces or lines where the mnemonic suggestions should be. After sympathizing a bit with them about how hard it is to tell the words apart when they look and sound so much alike, ask them if they have developed any personal ways of distinguishing the words in the groups.

Let this lead to a discussion of mnemonic devices, and write *mnemonic* on the board, saying that it is itself a word that often stumps great spellers. Tell them that it derives from the Greek goddess of memory, Mnemosyne (pronounced ni-MAH-suh-nee).

Finally, go through the list and see how many mnemonic devices the class can come up with for the words on the list. Suggest some of your own or some of the ones above, but let students choose their own and record them so that they end up with a personal list of mnemonic devices.

Answers

Page 58, Maze
The shortest path to the finish passes through: 1. I hope that **we'll** win the game today. **2.** I am much taller **than** Margaret. **3.** I remember just **where** I left it! **4. Let's** be sure the store is open. **5.** I hope he doesn't **lose** his temper. **6.** I didn't **quite** understand your question. **7.** I'm so tired that I need to take a **break**. **8.** Do you know **where** this bus stops next? **9.** We spread **coarse** salt on the icy driveway. **10. Were** you there when I sang my solo? **11.** Now **let's** see if my mother will let me go. **12.** Of **course** your hair looks nice that way. **13.** The house was old but seemed **quite** sturdy. **14.** How **well** does he speak Spanish? **15.** My dog is **loose** in the backyard. **16.** Can we go **through** here? **17.** Here is a large **piece** of pie.

Page 59, Solve the Riddle
1. quite, where, through **2.** break, loose **3.** Let's, then, course **4.** peace, quiet, lose **5.** We're, lets **6.** brake, quiet **7.** piece, quite, than **8.** threw, piece, coarse, then
Answer: One is sick to quit, and one is quick to sit.

Maze

Directions: Find the path to the finish by passing through 17 words in **bold** that are correctly spelled. You cannot pass through a solid line or a space containing an incorrectly spelled word.

Hint: The **bold** words are all listed in the box below, but you must decide which similar spelling fits the meaning of the sentence in each space.

brake	coarse	lets	lose	piece	quite	then	threw	well	were
break	course	let's	loose	peace	quiet	than	through	we'll	we're
									where

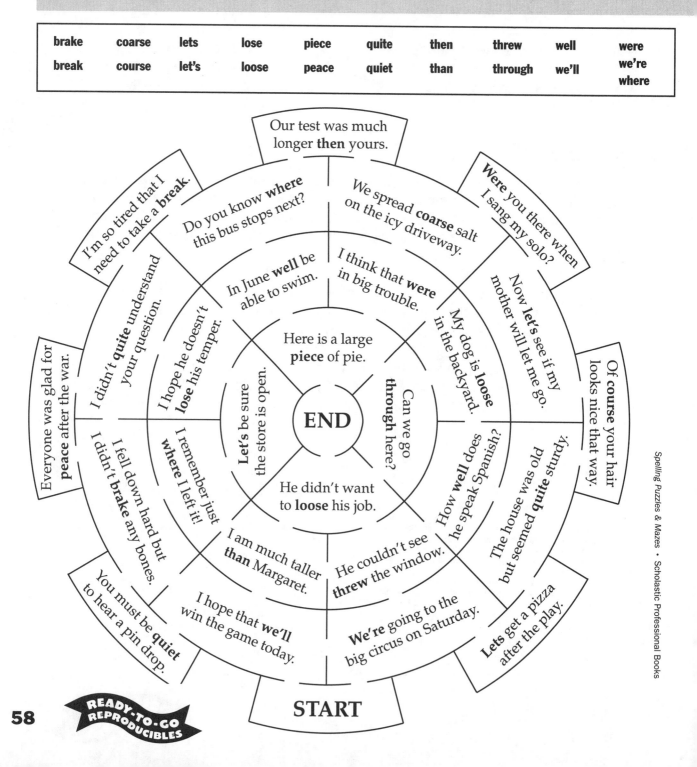

Our test was much longer **then** yours.

I'm so tired that I need to take a **break**.

Do you know **where** this bus stops next?

We spread **coarse** salt on the icy driveway.

Were you there when I sang my solo?

In June **well** be able to swim.

I think that **were** in big trouble.

Now **let's** see if my mother will let me go.

I didn't **quite** understand your question.

I hope he doesn't **lose** his temper.

Here is a large **piece** of pie.

My dog is **loose** in the backyard.

Of **course** your hair looks nice that way.

Everyone was glad for **peace** after the war.

Let's be sure the store is open.

END

Can we go **through** here?

I fell down hard but I didn't **brake** any bones.

I remember just **where** I left it!

He didn't want to **loose** his job.

How **well** does he speak Spanish?

The house was old but seemed **quite** sturdy.

You must be **quiet** to hear a pin drop.

I am much taller **than** Margaret.

I hope that **we'll** win the game today.

He couldn't see **threw** the window.

We're going to the big circus on Saturday.

Lets get a pizza after the play.

START

READY-TO-GO REPRODUCIBLES

Spelling Puzzles & Mazes • Scholastic Professional Books

Name_____ Date _____

Solve the Riddle

What is the difference between a student who has to stop playing an exciting game and a student who rips the seat of his pants?

Directions: To answer the riddle, first choose the correctly spelled word in each set of parentheses. Then for each correct word, write the underlined letter in the matching answer space. The first one has been done for you.

brake	coarse	lets	lose	piece	quite	then	threw	were
break	course	let's	loose	peace	quiet	than	through	we're
								where

1. I'm ((quite), quiet) sure that I know (we**re**, whe**re**) we can get (th**r**ew, thro**u**gh) this fence.
　　　　8　　　14　　　　　　　　22　　　14　　　　　　6　　　　　9

2. Did the bear (brea**k**, b**r**ake) (lo**o**se, **l**ose) from his cage?
　　　　　　　　19　12　　　1　　3

3. (Le**t**s, Let'**s**) have a salad and (**t**han, the**n**) share the main (co**u**rse, coa**r**se).
　　20　　　4　　　　　　　　8　　　13　　　　　　　16　　　21

4. The chess player begged, "I need some (**p**iece, pea**c**e) and (q**u**ite, qui**e**t) or I'll (loo**s**e, lo**s**e)
　　　　　　　　　　　　　　　　18　　　　6　　　3　　　17　　　　　2　　12

my concentration."

5. (We**r**e, We'r**e**) happy that the coach (let**s**, let'**s**) us quit early on Fridays.
　　8　　　3　　　　　　　　　20　　7

6. The warning buzzer for our car's emergency (b**r**eak, bra**k**e) is too (**q**uiet, qui**t**e).
　　　　　　　　　　　　　　13　　　7　　　　　15　　　4

7. This (p**i**ece, pea**c**e) of pizza looks (qui**e**t, qu**i**te) big, but it's really no bigger (**t**hen, tha**n**) yours.
　　5　　　14　　　　　　　　1　　　10　　　　　　　　　　22　　　2

8. The chef (th**r**ew, throu**g**h) a huge (pea**c**e, p**i**ece) of (**c**oarse, cou**r**se) pepper into the pot
　　11　　　15　　　　　　6　　　21　　　18　　　11

and (**t**han, the**n**) smiled wickedly.
　　19　　22

Answer:

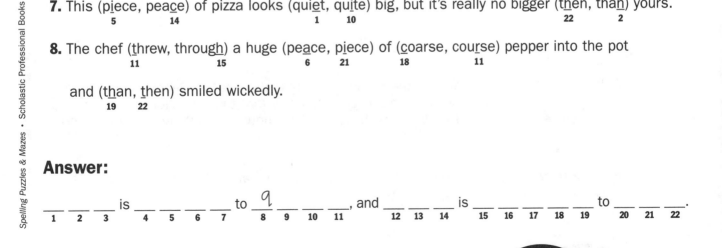

__ __ __ is __ __ __ __ to _9_ __ __ __ , and __ __ __ is __ __ __ __ __ to __ __ __ .
1　2　3　　4　5　6　7　　8　9　10　11　　12　13　14　　15　16　17　18　19　　20　21　22

Unit 13: Similar Endings: -ous, -us, -cal, -cle, -ful

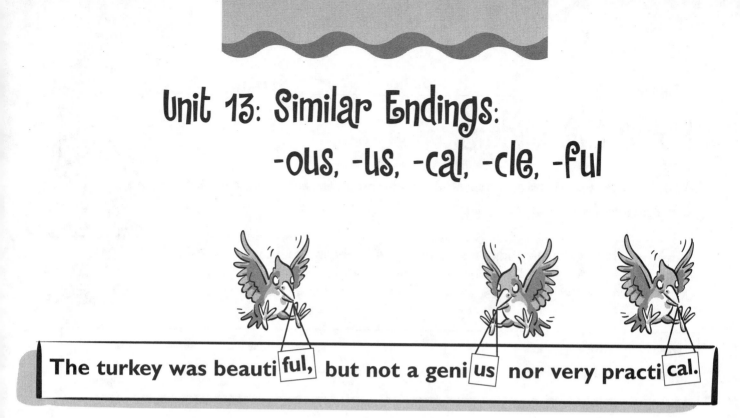

The turkey was beauti|ful,| but not a geni|us| nor very practi|cal.|

While English is notorious for its spelling irregularities and exceptions, there are a few patterns that, if recognized, can put a little more method into the seeming madness. This unit isolates three patterns that will help students choose the correct endings for frequently misspelled words like *genius* and *envious, comical* and *obstacle,* and words that end in *-ful.*

Similar Ending Rules:

1. The *-ous* ending is used for *adjectives*; the *-us* ending is used for *nouns.*

2. The *-cal* ending is used for *adjectives*; the *-cle* ending is used for *nouns.*

3. The only word ending in *full* is the word *full* itself; all others end in *-ful.*

Teaching Tip

☀ If students can't remember if the proper spelling is *identi**cal*** or *identi**cle***, they need only recognize that *identical* is an adjective to know that the first choice is correct. Is *octopus* spelled correctly here? Yes, because it's a noun and thus ends with *-us,* not *-ous.*

Exception to the rule: A few nouns, such as *rascal,* end in *-al,* and the words *musical* and *radical* can be nouns as well as adjectives.

Spelling Puzzles & Mazes • Scholastic Professional Books

Mini-Lesson

Once they've learned the rules above, students can apply them quite easily—as long as they can identify adjectives and nouns. But the identification of parts of speech is, as every English teacher knows, difficult for many students, even after many years of instruction and drill. Before setting out on the exercises that follow, it may be helpful to have students practice spotting nouns and adjectives.

The old definition of nouns as names of persons, places, or things is helpful, but many of the "things" that nouns name are abstractions—*source, happiness, reality*—that don't seem very "thingy." One way to test if a word is a noun is to try to put the word *the* or *my* before it. Since *the* is an article and *my* is a possessive (in effect, an adjective), then words they modify will be (or will function as) nouns: Can you say *the source*? *my happiness*? Yes, these are nouns. But you couldn't say *the comical*. It isn't a noun. This test can be used to pick out the words that should end in *-us* and *-cle*—*the article* but not *the practical*; *the octopus* but not *the fabulous*.

When you have students decide if a word is a noun or an adjective, be sure to use the words in sentences and check that you haven't inadvertently used one of the nouns in an adjective slot—*She was wearing an octopus suit.*

Answers

Page 62, Hidden Message
Correctly spelled words: 1. critical **2.** bicycle **3.** comical **4.** particle **5.** magical **6.** obstacle **7.** spectacle **8.** mystical **9.** logical **10.** icicle **11.** useful **12.** awful **13.** helpful **14.** hopeful **15.** fruitful **16.** powerful **17.** skillful **18.** artful **19.** plentiful **20.** walrus **21.** vigorous **22.** genius **23.** dangerous **24.** radius **25.** delicious **26.** glorious **27.** fabulous **28.** circus **29.** tremendous
Message: HELP

Page 63, Maze
The shortest path to the finish passes through: 1. spectacle **2.** typical **3.** article **4.** full **5.** obvious **6.** beautiful **7.** tremendous **8.** critical **9.** helpful **10.** genius
Bonus: 6, Start, Finish, glorious, useful, fanciful, walrus

Page 64, Message in a Grid
1. nervous **2.** genius, mournful **3.** logical, practical **4.** envious **5.** critical, useful, hopeful **6.** icicle **7.** tremendous, obstacle, powerful **8.** wonderful, circus, walrus, humorous **9.** spectacle, typical
Grid key: MARIE (humorous, obstacle, walrus, critical, wonderful); AND (practical, mournful, tremendous); PIERRE (hopeful, logical, useful, circus, nervous, spectacle); CURIE (icicle, envious, powerful, typical, genius)
Message: Marie and Pierre Curie

Name_____ Date _____

Hidden Message

Lori Goodwin, a night superintendent, was in charge of heating, cooling, and lighting a skyscraper. One night, in the control room, she slipped and injured her leg so that she couldn't get to the phone. Luckily, she was next to the lighting control panel, and thinking fast, she switched off the lights in certain rooms to spell out a message. Within minutes, emergency workers came to her rescue and helped her get to a hospital.

Directions: To find out what Lori's message was, circle only the correctly spelled words in the lists below. Then, darken the squares in the skyscraper grid that match the number-letter pairs next to each of the correctly spelled words. The first one has been done for you.

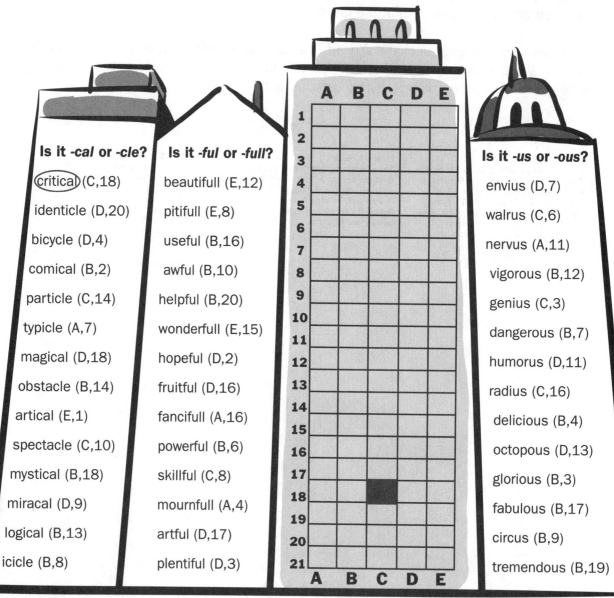

Is it -cal or -cle?

critical (C,18)

identicle (D,20)

bicycle (D,4)

comical (B,2)

particle (C,14)

typicle (A,7)

magical (D,18)

obstacle (B,14)

artical (E,1)

spectacle (C,10)

mystical (B,18)

miracal (D,9)

logical (B,13)

icicle (B,8)

Is it -ful or -full?

beautifull (E,12)

pitifull (E,8)

useful (B,16)

awful (B,10)

helpful (B,20)

wonderfull (E,15)

hopeful (D,2)

fruitful (D,16)

fancifull (A,16)

powerful (B,6)

skillful (C,8)

mournfull (A,4)

artful (D,17)

plentiful (D,3)

Is it -us or -ous?

envius (D,7)

walrus (C,6)

nervus (A,11)

vigorous (B,12)

genius (C,3)

dangerous (B,7)

humorus (D,11)

radius (C,16)

delicious (B,4)

octopous (D,13)

glorious (B,3)

fabulous (B,17)

circus (B,9)

tremendous (B,19)

Maze

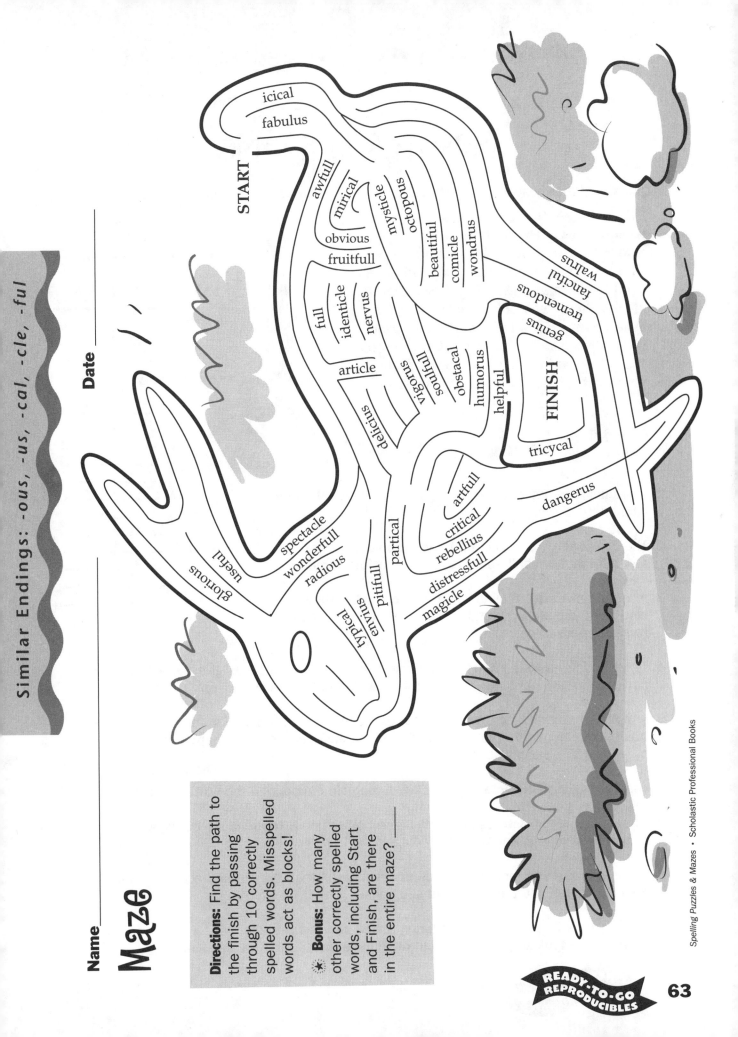

Directions: Find the path to the finish by passing through 10 correctly spelled words. Misspelled words act as blocks!

✷ **Bonus:** How many other correctly spelled words, including Start and Finish, are there in the entire maze? ____

START

icical
fabulus

awfull
mirical
obvious
fruitfull

mysticle
octopous
beautiful
comicle
wondrus

full
identicle
nervus

article

delicius
vigorus
soulfull

fanciful
walrus

tremendous

obstacal
humorus

genius

helpful

FINISH

tricycal

artfull
critical
rebellius
distressfull
magicle

dangerus

partical
pitifull
envius
typical

radious
wonderfull
spectacle
useful
glorious

Name_____ Date _____

Message in a Grid

Question: What husband and wife team, working in France, discovered radioactivity?

Directions: You can answer this question—or check your answer if you think you already know it—by correctly spelling words that end in -cal and -cle, -ous and -us, and -ful. Some of the words in **bold** are spelled correctly and some are spelled incorrectly. Identify and then place the correctly spelled words into the grid. When all the words are inserted, the answer to the question will appear in the vertical boxes.

Hint: Use the letters that are already in place and leave no box empty. Each answer will fit exactly on one line of the grid.

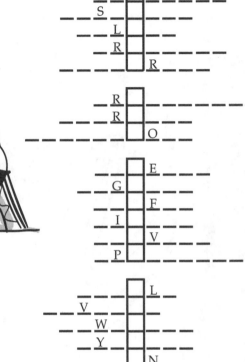

1. I was **nervous** before my vaccination, but a **helpfull** nurse calmed me down.

2. The composer was supposed to be a **genius**, but her **mournful** music didn't seem right in a **musicle** comedy.

3. Inventors must be imaginative and **fancifull**, but they also have to be **logical**, stubborn, and **practical** if their inventions are to get sold.

4. Tanya wasn't **envious** when her **identicle** twin sister Therese was given a **glorius** necklace for their birthday, for she got a **fabulus** new **bicycal**.

5. Although the newspapers were **critical** of the mayor's **ambitius** plan for new commuter trains, the commuters thought that it was a **useful** idea and were **hopeful** that it would be adopted by the city council.

6. The long, **beautifull icicle** gleamed like a **magicle** diamond in the winter sunshine.

7. By conquering my **distressfull** stage fright, I overcame a **tremendous obstacle** to my becoming a **vigorus** and **powerful** actor.

8. To me, the zoo was more **delightfull** and **wonderful** than the **circus** because of the **comicle walrus** and the **humorous** sea lions.

9. The ice show seemed like a **dangerus, artfull spectacle** to me, but for the performers it was just a **typical** show, filled with ordinary leaps and routine dances.

Spelling Puzzles & Mazes • Scholastic Professional Books